AGE OF HEROES

γένος των ἥρώων

AGE OF HEROES

Beyond the Solar Path

Written by Tom Billinge

Published by Sanctus Europa Press

Paperback: 978-1-7362937-4-4

Hardcover: 978-1-7362937-5-1

Library of Congress Number pending.

Editing and layout by Benjamin Sieghart.

Cover art (*Odysseus and the Sea Nymphs* and back cover) by Skinless Frank.

Inside illustrations (*The Dancing Warrior*, *Homer*, *Akhilleus*, and *Odysseus*) by Ben Ervin.

Inside map taken from the public domain.

More at:

tombillinge.com

sanctuseuropa.com

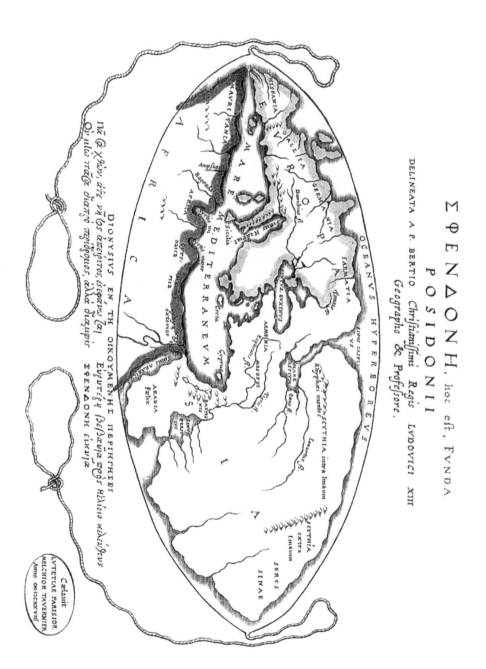

Map of the World (according to Posidonius), c. 1st Century BCE.

Table of Contents

"Always be the best, hold your head up high above the others. Never shame the line of your ancestors."

Iliad

Acknowledgements

This book is the culmination of a lifelong love of the most ancient and holy works of European culture: the *Iliad* and *Odyssey*. These two books have come down to us almost unchanged through the mists of time in spite of changing ethics, rulership, and religious sentiment. They have encouraged countless generations to be heroes. The gods, muses, and poets who inspired and channelled the ancestral songs are owed my first offering of gratitude.

My love for the Homeric works was furthered by both my mother and my father. My mother, Anastasia, was Greek-Cypriot and her love of her family, people, and culture was infectious. She made sure that my siblings and I knew who we were, where we were from, and the lineage that lead to us. Thanks to her, I know my ancestors.

My father, Mark, is a retired lecturer in historical geography at the University of Cambridge. He always encouraged any interests his children held, but mine was particularly close to home for him. He took me on his field trips to Crete when I was a child and fostered my love of archaeology and mythology. He aided me every step of the way through my academic career, particularly when I was writing both my Sixth Form and University theses on Alexander the Great and Minoan Cretan archaeology respectively.

My editor, Benjamin Sieghart, has been invaluable as always. His understanding of the esoteric is unrivalled by anyone I have met. He challenges and encourages in equal measure, making him the ideal man to shape my roughly hewn creations into works worthy of public scrutiny.

My wife, Kristin, through her support, makes my work possible. Words are insufficient to express my deep gratitude, respect, and love for her.

This book is dedicated to the heroes. The world needs you.

Notes on Language

As with my previous work *Undying Glory*, I have in most cases utilised a transliterative spelling of Homeric Greek. Many spellings from works the non-Greek reader is accustomed to are Latinised. The Romans replaced the letter "k" with "c," which does not exist in the Greek alphabet. The letter "i" was often replaced with an "e," and the letter "o" with a "u" also. For example, the Greek name "Menelaos" is rendered Meneleus and the place name "Phaiakia" is Phaeacia in the Latin spelling.

The more accurate Greek spellings in *Age of Heroes* are an attempt to familiarise readers with the original pronunciations of names and concepts. Some examples of this spelling system are:

"Akhaians" for Achaeans
"Akhilleus" for Achilles
"Aias" for Ajax
"Mykenai" for Mycenae
"Krete" for Crete
"Ithake" for Ithaca
"Kyklopes" for Cyclopes

There are some instances where this rule is not followed, as it would confuse the reader (for example, centaur is not rendered "kentauros"). There are others, however, where I have maintained the original spelling of words rather than trying to phoneticise them. I've done this in cases where the letter "u" can be pronounced in Greek as a "y" or an "f." For example:

Kûdos is pronounced *"kydos"*
Thumós is pronounced *"thymos"*
Húbris is pronounced *"hybris"*
Zeus is pronounced "Zefs"
Odysseus is pronounced "Odyssefs"

The Greek language also does not contain a letter "w," but it once did. The digamma (rendered "Ϝ" in Greek) was used in Mykenaian Greek and will appear in the Mykenaians chapter of this book. The Mykenaians would have known Troy or Ilion as "Wilion" or "Wilios," which is closer to the Hittite name for the city: Wilusa. In later Greek the digamma was dropped, rendering words like *wánax* (lord) as *"ánax."*

The word *génos* (γένος) literally translates to "generation" or "race" but is commonly rendered "age" in English. Therefore, *Khrysó Génos* (Χρυσό Γένος) would translate to "Golden Race," but I have rendered it as "Golden Age" to better convey its meaning in the context of this work.

Prologue

The previous book, *Undying Glory*, saw the completion of the "Solar Path" by the hero Herakles. This work takes up where *Undying Glory* finished with the next generation of heroes, and the possibility of going beyond the Solar Path to the "Polar Ascent." The Solar Path is reiterated with the hero Akhilleus; but the hero Odysseus shows us a continued route that goes further, taking the hero home to the North.

This book sets the premise for a new Age of Heroes that is imminent. Another generation of heroes will once again strive to make the world in their image, but also do the inner work required to transcend from warriors to true heroes.

Undying Glory left off with Herakles becoming an Olympian. He completed the first level of the inner work and overcame death, making himself an equal of the gods. As the man-born son of Zeus and prototypical Solar Hero, he achieved the *"atidevic"* state without having to embark on the journey's next phase. He is unique in this, however.

Age of Heroes continues this quest through those who followed the earlier generation. They are the heroes who fought at Thebes and Troy and are documented in the Greek Epic Cycle, of which only the *Iliad* and *Odyssey* remain in totality.

Undying Glory was the first initiatory level of the heroic path of *atideva* (the state beyond the gods). *Age of Heroes* is the second degree of initiation. The third and final stage comes after this current work.

In order to ascend the Hyperborean pinnacle, it is necessary to go through the levels of initiation. There are no shortcuts, but the ancients left clues in their works. The fragmentary directions can still lead the warrior to become a hero, the hero to become a god, and the god to transcend the bounds of time and space.

Introduction

"Now these things never happened, but always are."
Saloustios

The Greek Age of Heroes was immortalised in the epic canon, of which two works by a poet named Homer survive. The *Iliad* tells the tale of a few days during the siege of the city of Ilion (or Troy). The *Odyssey* narrates the journey home of the hero Odysseus.

Archaeologists and historians have spent centuries trying to square up the Homeric epics with the Greek and Anatolian Bronze Age. Philologists, mythographers, and classicists have argued over the identity and existence of Homer. All these scholars have spent countless hours attempting to prove or debunk aspects of the stories and their attributed author.

This book does not add to the arguments of any side of scholastic thought. This work is for the heroes; it is for the men of this world attempting to navigate their way through this Age of Iron in which we find ourselves today. For those striving toward a new Heroic Age, it gazes back upon the last for guidance and encouragement.

While we can acknowledge there was a Trojan War in the Bronze Age (as archaeology suggests), we cannot use the *Iliad* and *Odyssey* as historically accurate documents of that conflict. They are mythopoetic oral transmissions from generations of Akhaian Greeks. The actions of the Greek Bronze Age heroes were absorbed into a greater narrative, the Indo-European heroic mythos, leaving the works that survive today.

Homer sings of a rougher, more elemental time before the Mykenaian palaces. The poems incorporate deep time and retrospect. These tales of Greeks before they were Greek were recollected in the relative tranquillity of 1300 BCE, then written down in 750 BCE when writing first truly existed in Greece. They are the Greeks' deep memories of their Indo-European past.

The poems embody what is always true, not just what was true then. They give us values and ethics that remain perennial in the face of inconstant and unproven cultural norms. They take place in mythic time, the strong time.

They are ageless, stretching across all epochs – ancient to the ancients. They embody timeless otherness. Impolite, manly, cosmic, wild, enormous, the subject is not elegance, but beauty and truth.

Historians and classicists might tell you that Homer is said to have come from Smyrna or Khios in Asia Minor. They may also tell you that Homer did not exist, and that the oral poems were the assembled and collected works of several poets. They may even say that they were not oral at all, and committed to paper from the outset.

The hero understands Homer is the spirit of the poetry itself: its *daímōn*. Homer is the poetry. He is from nowhere and everywhere – the *daímōn* of the ancient song of the Indo-European people.

Aristotle reports that Homer was born from a spirit, a *daímōn*, who danced with the muses. Plutarch says Homer was born of Kalliope ("Beautiful Voice"), the muse of epic and daughter of Zeus and Mnemosyne ("Memory"). This implies Homer's words are descended from Olympian power and memory – they are words and recollections of gods on high.

The name Homer could mean "blind," "connector," "bond," or "hostage." However, it is his hidden name Melesignes ("caring for his clan") which matters most. This hidden name is of one who cares for his people and their heroic inheritance.

He presents them with his *Kósmos*, a word meaning "order," "world," "beauty," and "honour." Everything associated with the heroic (nobility, directness, vitality, truth, courage, adventure) are all aspects of the Cosmic. This is precisely what Homer embodies.

The poet is a seer, able to comprehend beyond human limitations. He invokes the muses in order to transport his consciousness through time and space. This is how he can witness the deeds of great heroes and act as their voice.

He calls upon the gods and heroes, summoning them into the present, and makes their presence felt. Inspired by the Muses (also children of Memory), the Greek poet-seer gives voice to this bygone Age of Heroes. The ancestral memory of a deep past is channelled through the singer, giving form to the epic.

The gift of the muses is true speech and Apollon, Lord of the Muses, loves truth above all things. The epic is a vehicle carrying truth and meaning from past into present over the yawning chasm of time. The poet is a medium for the old Heroic Age to spring forth into present; he is the spark that can light the flame of a new Age of Heroes.

Only if the tale resists the erosions of time can it be a vehicle of *Kléos Áphthiton* (Undying Glory). This Undying Glory is both the epic's substance and purpose. The greatest prize a hero can win is a place in the song. Honour exists in both the tale and its telling.

The story is both alive and fixed, composition and memory. The world forgets, but the poem remembers – and only the gods know as much as the poem. The poem is a magic spell, an enchantment; it is a holy work which can invoke an ancestral power in the hearts of men today. It makes us yearn for a new Age of Heroes.

The epics of Homer were possibly committed to memory by rhapsodes, and in particular a school of poets on the island of Khios called the Homeridai, who claimed Homer as their ancestor. The texts were slightly altered in places, and the first "definitive edition" was commissioned by the tyrant Pisistratos of Athens in the mid to late 6th century BCE. Pisistratos may have invited one of the Homeridai to recite the poems to a scribe.

Epic is the song and rhetoric of kings and heroes. Democracy brought a more technical, but less dignified form of poetry. The poet became secularised, no longer divine.

Other epic poems telling tales of the heroes of the Theban and Trojan wars were committed to paper at the same time. These are collectively known as the Epic Cycle. The librarians at Alexandria did some editing on the full Epic Cycle to make it fit into a unified body of work, but for the most part the *Iliad* and *Odyssey* were kept intact. The works were then meticulously copied by hand over the centuries and into the Christian era.

Due to the immense work required, only what was seen as worthwhile to the scribes was copied. The Homerica was deemed valuable (despite its pagan nature) when other works were discarded, including the remaining eight poems of the Epic Cycle. Much of this body of work was lost with the destruction of the Alexandria Library and sack of Byzantium. The oldest complete manuscripts of Homeric poems are from the 14th and 15th centuries CE. They have not, however, been altered in any significant way.

The Homeric poems have survived through millennia because they take place in cyclical, not linear time, and portray what is always true on a mythical level. They are an ancestral inheritance that runs deep, resonating with all European people. The poems of Homer constitute the root of Western Culture; if European history begins with the Greeks, Greek history begins with the world of Homer.

The deep layers of the epic have been replayed in all heroic times – from the foundation of the Roman Empire, to the fight back of Alfred and the Saxons, to the insurgency of the American Revolution. The ancestors of the Celts and Germanic people were also part of the Indo-European invasion of Europe (of which Homer's work is a reverberation). This is why the heroic figures of Irish, Germanic, and Caucasus sagas seem so similar to the characters in the poetry of Homer.

What is powerful about the Homeric works is that they were the first of the European heroic inheritance committed to paper. Homer's language – like that of the Greek Bronze Age – is still spoken recognisably in Greece today, almost unchanged since the second millennium BCE. A Greek can read the works in their original language without need of translation.

No other literary figure has held such a position in the life of his people as Homer. The narratives were of the highest social importance and were believed implicitly by the ancient Greeks. No Greek doubted there had been an Age of Heroes. Plato in the *Republic* put forward Homer as the model for cultural and human affairs.

When the poems were first being committed to paper in the 8th century BCE, archaeology shows disturbance at the Bronze Age sites. The Greeks of the Dark Age were using the old Mykenaian sites for ritual purpose. The surge of oral heroic poetry and desire to record it for future generations coincided with a ritualising of ancient sites associated with the heroes. These poems were not mere entertainment to the Greeks, but religious verse that resonated with a fallen group of people seeking to regain their former glory.

We must do the same. We must seek to start a new Age of Heroes and gain our own Undying Glory. This begins by retelling the epic tales of our greatest forebears.

Steppe Warband vs the World

The *Iliad* preserves in its layers the most ancient strata of Indo-European warrior mythology. The language of the pastoral Steppe in Homer stands in sharp contrast to that of the agrarian city-state, which defines the Biblical Old Testament. The mythos of a cattle raiding "männerbund" is present throughout the *Iliad*; it sets mobile warbands against the city.

The Akhaians embody nomadic Steppe raiders – warriors of a pre-urban, pre-palatial time. The Trojans are Anatolian palace dwellers, embodying a settled Indo-European people like the Hittites, who adopted Babylonian and Akkadian ways of living. There is a deep memory of the later Greek wave of Indo-European people encountering previous waves, their vassal people, and their cities. The *Iliad* is filled with these buried recollections.

The Trojans are heroic adversaries because they share the Indo-European Steppe ancestry. However, they are enemies because they are urbanised. These once noble people have been corrupted by Southern and Near Eastern ways.

The *Iliad* never visits Greece, but is always set in the Near East. The Greeks talk of their families and land, but never of cities. They are loosely affiliated warrior bands attacking a centrally governed city people.

The Greeks have blonde hair, the Trojans' is dark. Troy represents the Near Eastern city with its taxed, state-controlled, and urbane human herd. They are ripe for raiding by the undomesticated Steppe warrior band.

The nomadic warrior gang is pitted against the city. The Trojans are the urbanised, weaker, decadent people. The Greeks are purer, more savage. The city weakens man; the lures of its delights soften him, making him more pliable and distracted. Paris, for example, is an urban dandy – a feminised, woman-crazed pretty-boy with no heart for the fight.

The Greeks are the side of Tradition fighting against cosmopolitan forces of "progress" embodied in the morally declining city of Troy. The Near Eastern lure of urban comfort, servitude, profit, regulation, and centralised authority creates a race of weak men. This is what Troy ultimately represents.

Twenty percent of the Homeric material is in pre-Linear B Greek, making it extremely ancient – far older than the Mykenaian Bronze Age. Homer gives voice to the Northern warrior culture of the Steppe. He animates a mobile, violent, masculine, meat-eating, war-focussed elite with no permanent settlements.

Their fundamental opposition to the Southern cities of the Eastern Mediterranean is made tangible through his song. Song is central to the warrior complex, and Homer is the only place we can hear the voices of these ancient warriors. It offers us a direct connection to the heroic world: the realm of gang violence and poetry.

The Cattle Raid

At the heart of the Indo-European mythos is the cattle raid. The youthful warband roams the Steppe rustling cattle and taking women as brides. The raid is met with counter-raid, where cattle and women are stolen back. Sometimes this myth involves a prize cow being stolen and the warrior band attacking the thieving tribe to take it back, but exacting complete revenge by taking all their cattle wealth.

Greek mythology is filled with echoes of the cattle raid. Herakles steals the cattle of Geryon; Nestor raids the cattle of the sun; the Dioskouroi steal both the brides and cattle of their cousins the Apharetidai. This world of cattle raiding and chariot warfare becomes more expansive over time. Originally it is just cattle, but eventually cattle, horses, women, metals, weapons, and other things of value are sought out.

The *Iliad* also paints a mythical portrait of the cattle raid and its aftermath. A band of heroes get together to enact retribution by taking back from another band of heroes what was stolen from them – and more. The text is permeated with cattle and horse references.

Raiding, sacrifice, feast, and distribution are continually reinforced. This is the way of life of the Akhaians. The theft of a royal bride, a chieftain's wife, is what starts the conflict.

This is a continuation of the Indo-European cattle raid, which serves as part of their origin story. First, man sacrifices his twin or a cow. His herd is then stolen by a serpent, and he retrieves the cattle with the help of the Striker god, of whom Zeus is an echo (along with the Sky Father).

The Greeks seek to take back Helen, wife of Menelaos, along with all bride wealth taken with her by Paris to Troy. Helen is also a reverberation of the rape of Kore, the maiden goddess. Hades steals Kore-Persephone, taking her to the Underworld. Theseus abducts Helen when she is a young girl before her brothers steal her back. This is connected in the Theseus mythology to the hero and his ally Peirithoos attempting to take Persephone from Hades.

Helen was always a goddess to the Spartans, descendants of the Akhaians of Sparta ruled by Menelaos. One of the conditions for sacking Troy is that the Akhaians must steal from the city the Palladion statue, an image of the goddess Athena. These two acts – the theft of the Palladion and recovery of Helen – are intrinsically entwined.

Troy is referred to as a holy city (Sacred Ilios), the city east of the sun and west of the moon. It is home to the Palladion statue, a token of the goddess protector's patronage. In some ways, this potent symbol of power is the true quest of the Akhaians. The thefts of this goddess and her power are one and the same.

The cattle raid also shapes much of the *Odyssey*, with the cattle and flocks of the sun appearing both explicitly and implicitly throughout the tale. The cattle of the sun lived on the periphery of the Greek cosmos. They symbolised the heart of the Greek sacrifice: the animals that defined their relationship with the gods. This is explored more deeply in the *Odyssey*.

The Liquid Steppe

The *Odyssey* brings us to another phase of the heroic period. The people who would become the Greeks were strangers to the southern sea. They were northerners from the steppelands of Eurasia: landlocked, dominated by an eternal blue sky, horse-rich, concerned with herds and flocks, meat-fuelled, violent, mobile, heroic.

When they encountered the sea, they did so head-on, indomitably. They built ships and rode them as sea chariots on the liquid steppe. The poet of the *Odyssey* says of the Phaiakian vessel: "The ship – like four yoked stallions on the plain that spring forward together under the whip's strokes, and swiftly, high-stepping, gallop upon their way – likewise lifted her stern." In the poem, Penelope also describes ships as "swift-moving vessels that serve mankind as the sea's horses."

The *Odyssey* takes the mobile warband onto the waters where they set sail, finding new settled people to raid and interact with. The cattle raid is ever-present in the poem, and frequently referenced. The herdsmen of Odysseus have high status positions, reinforcing the proto-Greek and Indo-European Steppe culture.

However, the *Odyssey* takes us beyond the Steppe. It sends us on both an inner and outer journey through strange lands exterior to the realm of Olympian gods. Present throughout are the herds of Helios, Titanic god of the sun and true antagonist of Odysseus.

The *Odyssey* is an upwardly transcendent addition to the heroic groundwork laid in the *Iliad*. They form a complimentary pair. The *Iliad* is horizontal, the *Odyssey* vertical; the *Iliad* is oriented east, the *Odyssey* west. The *Iliad* is red, fire, and earth; the *Odyssey* is purple, wind, and the sea.

The *Iliad* is retrospect, and the *Odyssey* possibilities of forward-facing adventure. The *Iliad* deals with the demands of fate; the *Odyssey* shows the hero standing against fate. The Odyssean promise of transcendence tempers the Iliadic certainty of death.

They teach us about *moîra* ("fate"): a force independent of the gods, ruling the course of men's lives and determining when we die. We learn we cannot escape our allotted time of death, but can choose how we live. We may decide to be filled with *sébas* ("awe"), facing the gods heroically and seeking the eternal.

We can see the *enárgeia* ("bright, vivid reality"), the form of the gods without disguise. When perfection is attained as the circle closes at the moment of death, we can meet it gloriously. We can attain *kalós thánatos* ("a beautiful death").

While death for these heroes brings an end to their Age, their stories live on. Their struggles to attain fame, glory, and transcendence enter into sacred, strong time. The repetition of the divine model maintains the sanctity of the world.

These poems are not in the past, but now. They are timeless, forever, true. They are a bright and shining ideal which renders unbearable our dark, sullied reality.

γένη των ανθρώπων

Ages of Men

Hesiod's *Works and Days* is the main Greek source for the pan-Indo-European concept of Ages of Men. Written in the 8th Century BCE, the poem expresses a much more ancient concept. Both the Vedic and Avestan canons also expound an idea of cyclic time with a distinct recycling of ages. This *anakýklosis* ("recycling") turns through four main ages in the Indic tradition, but five in the Greek.

There is a direct correspondence between the Greek and Indic ages. The Greek Golden Age (χρυσό γένος) corresponds to the Indic Age of Truth (Satya Yuga), the Silver Age (αργυρό γένος) to the Age of the Three (Treta Yuga), the Bronze Age (χάλκινο γένος) to the Age of the Two (Dvapara Yuga), and the Age of Iron (γένος του σιδήρου) to the Age of Darkness (Kali Yuga).

While the Indic tradition does not have a separate and specific Age of Heroes (γένος των ἡρώων), each age is preceded by a dawn (Sandhya) and dusk (Sandhyansa). These dawns and dusks suggest each age has a period of adjustment and change directly before and after its advent, which ties into the Greek concept of an Age of Heroes.

These Heroic Ages are interludes that open and close each of the four Ages of Men in a perpetual cycle, known to Plato as the "Great Year." A full turn of a Great Year includes a cycle of each of the Ages of Men.

Golden Age

Men of the first age (of the Titan Kronos) were fashioned of gold. They knew no suffering and honoured the gods. When their mortal life ended, they became pure spirits who dwell in nature.

These men lived like gods in an age of kings – of paternal solar regality. It was a time when Kronos was ruler of the heavens, before his son Zeus wrested power from him. Although the age began with Titanic rule, it was Olympian in nature, allowing Zeus to take his rightful place as ruler of the cosmos. Men and gods feasted together in the Golden Age. They knew each other's company and lived together in harmony.

The Golden Race lived carefree lives without pain, misery, or old age. They remained vigorous until they died. They never toiled on the land, as it provided its fruits without need for labour. Hesiod states that they "lived in peace and abundance as lords of their lands, rich in flocks and dear to the blessed gods." He also tells us that the earth covered this race and that they became benevolent spirits that walk the earth, watching over mortals.

Silver Age

The second race were of silver. Coddled and debased, they were witless and did not offer sacrifice to the gods. Still, they were honoured by the gods when they passed.

Men of the Silver Age lost their godlike heritage. Instead, they had a maternal, Demetrian, and priestly lunar spirituality. The Race of Silver were almost the opposite of the Golden Race. They were nurtured as children by their mothers for 100 years and did not live long after reaching adolescence.

They were violent against one another and refused to give *tīmaí* ("honours") to the gods. Zeus grew weary of them and buried them below ground. They became blessed chthonic spirits, living under the earth.

The dawn of the Silver Age is the time that Titan Prometheus settled the sacrificial rites with the gods on behalf of mankind. Tricking them into accepting the bones of a sacrificial victim instead of meat, Prometheus usurped some of the power of the gods for men. Since feasting and sacrifice are one and the same, division of meat and distribution of honours go hand-in-hand. The gods took their honours from the Titans by way of their might. When men failed to give honours to the gods, man's status lowered.

Thus, the Promethean settlement of the sacrifice began the decline of the state of man. The share of the sacrifice was no longer equal, so the schism began.

Bronze Age

The Bronze Race were warlike with immense strength. Through their own nature, they sent themselves into the underworld of Hades, the first dead to reside there.

Men of the Bronze Age loved nothing but war. They exhibited titanic traits like those of the giants. They practiced non-transcendent violence and conflict.

The Race of Bronze in Hesiod were fashioned from ash trees. In other accounts, they were the children of the Meliai ash tree nymphs, who were in turn children of the Earth Mother Gaia. They were a race of chthonic maternal violence – the quality of the god Ares, who was born of Hera alone without Zeus' seed.

These Bronze Age men were dreadful and mighty. They worked with bronze, using it for their weapons and houses.

They had hearts of steel and were strong and violent, killing each other off until only Talos remained. This last bronze man was killed by the witch Medeia when the Argonauts landed on Krete.

Age of Heroes

The fourth race were the heroic demigods. These were the men who fearlessly sought glory: the Akhaians who sailed to Troy and now dwell in the Isles of the Blessed, beside deep swirling Okeanos.

The Age of Heroes was a glimmer of the Golden Age. The heroes were created by Zeus, who gave them a spark of the Olympian flame. They contained the possibility of reattaining the primordial state and starting a new Golden Age, but were fated instead to commence the Age of Iron.

These heroes included Kadmos, Bellerophon, Perseus, Jason, Theseus, and Herakles. The next generation were the heroes who stormed Troy and laid siege to seven-gated Thebes. These were the last flicker of the possibilities of man.

Their fates differed; but after death, many went to live on the Isles of the Blessed, where they exist in bliss with others who lived and died heroically. Also known as Elysion, these Isles are ruled over by Kronos, father of Zeus. The Isles of the Blessed are a reflection of the Golden Age.

Age of Iron

We now live in the Age of Iron: an age of decline, where miscreant and thief are honoured above brother and comrade. Filled with strife, it is an age of deconsecrated civilisation, which knows and extolls only that which is human and earthly. The gods have been all but forgotten; heroism is rarely seen. This is the Kali Yuga.

Hesiod's description of the Age of Iron speaks for itself:

"Zeus will destroy this race of mortals when children are born grey at the temples. Children will not resemble their fathers, and there will be no affection between guest and host and no love between friends or brothers as in the past. Sons and daughters will be quick to offend their ageing parents and rebuke them and speak to them with rudeness and cruelty, not knowing about divine retribution; they will not even repay their parents for their keep – these law-breakers – and they will sack one another's city.

"The man who keeps his oath, or is just and good, will not be favoured, but the evildoers and scoundrels will be honoured, for might will make right and shame will vanish. Base men will harm their betters with words that are crooked and then swear they are fair. And all toiling humanity will be blighted with envy, grim and strident envy that takes its joy in the ruin of others." Hesiod, Works and Days (trans. Apostolos N. Athanakis)

This is our place among the Ages of Men, but all is not lost. We are on the brink of another Age of Heroes. The dusk of the Age of Iron is when, due to the gleam of gold within them, a new Race of Heroes has the chance to restart the Golden age.

Those of us who are capable must take action, beginning by walking the Solar Path to make ourselves into heroes through our sweat, blood, and tears. We must keep the fire burning and look to heroes who preceded us. This dark Age of Iron is unforgiving, but we must persevere.

We must pursue strength and integrity. We must honour the gods and our ancestors, but also work against the divine forces testing our resolve. Through this pressure we become diamonds gleaming in the next Golden Age. When the sun rises again, we can once more have direct knowledge of the gods in a primal state of Being.

ὁ ἥρωικό γένος

The Heroic Age

In the Great Cycle of time there have been several complete cycles through the Ages of Men. There have been other Ages of Heroes. The Greek Heroic Age songs were told to the military Mykenaian aristocracy in their language and terms, reflecting their world. These Bronze Age elites listened to the ancient tales and were inspired in the same way that Alexander, Caesar, and Alfred were by Homer's heroes.

The oldest strata of the Indo-European Age of Heroes has been relived and retold in each branch culture, resulting in the tales of Arthur, Sigurd, Cú Chulainn, and Batraz to name but a few. The themes remain true no matter the language and setting of the culture telling the tales. The Age of Heroes in Greek epic spanned a brief period of just two or three generations: from the founding of Thebes by Kadmos to the death of Odysseus.

The end of the Age of Heroes marked the beginning of the rise of soul over Spirit. It contained a gleam of the Golden Age, because within the Spirit of these heroes was a golden, divine spark. As the Age of Iron began however, the Spirit started giving ground to the lower soul. The involution of man, in a reflection of the Silver Age, began. The divine Spirit still remains in the men of today; but it is hidden, calcified with detritus, allowing the lower soul to be charioteer.

It is time for another Age of Heroes. Fresh songs need to be sung, but in order for that to happen, we must look back to the Homeric Age of Heroes for inspiration. We must remember that poetry is written in the blood of heroes.

The epics lay out a set of values coming to us from strong, mythical time. These values will once more become important as the Age of Iron gives way to another Age of Heroes. We must be inspired by the last – genuinely moved by its spirit and example. We must allow our instincts and imaginations to feed off its memory and energy.

We are currently deep into the fallen age. Lower even than an Age of Iron, we are in an Age of Lead. Rather than falling into despair, the hero understands that this is the ideal setting in which to rise. He knows that lead can be transmuted into gold.

The coming Age of Heroes can create a reaction so intense it resets the cycle, raising it from base matter to the pinnacle of gold. The Age of Heroes instigates a cultural war within the cosmic framework. It is able to shift the Great Cycle back to the start, returning gods and men into alignment.

The heroes bring this into reality through their willpower, refusing to consign themselves to fate. They embody the Western heroic archetype, acting against forces of fate, time, and the dissolutive powers of involution. By rejecting the cult of the mother that resigns itself to fate, the hero embraces the Olympian spirit. He is free from all constraints placed upon the ability to act.

The heroic way of life is suffocated in the modern, mechanised, spiritually impoverished world. Man's contact with his deep and free powers has been circumcised. Urban existence has petrified his heroic spirit, contaminating all aspects of his life. Feint-hearted ideologies of the weak foster nothing but pure contempt for heroic values.

The hero was the peak of hierarchy in ancient times. Today he is portrayed as a dangerous and harmful entity who needs to be summarily disposed of in the name of progress. But true heroes need to be made Self-aware once more.

They must move beyond the limits of materialism and reach higher in order to affect the changes that must come. Those who do not elevate themselves in this life will in death remain in the underground shadows. Only the few – the superior ones, the heroes – will ascend after their time on this mortal coil is complete.

The Hero

"He is a unique and isolated figure, whose arm is strong and deadly; he is devoted to combat, which he actively seeks out; he is detached from ordinary social space and is shown to be tremendously swift, able to cross time or the distance between worlds; and he is a very dangerous person in society and is therefore much better detached from it and sent away on a quest where he cannot harm ordinary mortals." Richard Harrison, Symbols and Warriors: Images of the European Bronze Age

The definition of "hero" has become muddied in the modern world. In order to dilute the true heroic spirit, anyone can be a hero for any reason. This egalitarian falsehood places all on the same level of achievement, which in turn aims to stop the true hero from rising.

Hero is a title of respect for those who accomplish. Heroes are a class of aristocracy: *āristoi* ("the best"), cognate with the pan-Indo-European word *árya* ("noble"). Hero and *árya* share a common Proto-Indo-European root *$h_2$eryós*.

A hero is a noble warrior with acknowledged victories. He belongs to the band of the best; comrades who also deserve fame and prizes: the *Prómachoi* ("those who fight from the front"). The hero is the strong among the strong.

The hero personifies beauty; his acts are acts of beauty. He is beautiful in body and Spirit, and seeks a beautiful death. He is pure.

The hero cannot submit to authority – it is not even a possibility for him. No satrap or over-king can exert his urban sovereignty over the hero. He is not a follower, but a leader; a trailblazer. He does not accept power that is bestowed by others, but seeks it out for himself and takes it with his own hands.

The hero is not only himself. He carries his entire ancestry and lineage on his shoulders. He is greater than one man, for he is the culmination of a long line that stretches back into ancient past.

The hero stands on the frontier of culture and nature. He knows that to die for something is better than to live for nothing. His greatness lies in his consciousness, in his capacity to act and comprehend both himself and his station at the same time. The hero is able to step back and conceive himself as immortal in Spirit while mortal in body.

The sphere of action is also of freedom, and this is where the hero resides. It is where he fully expresses himself. While his actions can be no higher than his understanding of the situation at hand, no explanation or justification is necessary in this realm. Societal values and norms do not restrain the hero's actions.

The actions of the hero appear as a form of madness to the outside observer. The hero's acts correspond to the rules of the heroic code: the sense of honour. Those not in this state of mind can only explain or justify the hero's actions, but never truly understand them. The outsider sees the acts as determined; the hero sees them as a perfect, free expression of his Self.

The hero recognises that his acts are final and unchangeable. He understands the ancient proverb that states one thing is beyond the power even of the gods: to make undone what has been done. He also knows the only constraint for action is the sphere of nature – that of forces.

Nature is the enduring order; the cosmos within which the hero acts. Within this sphere, men create their own destiny. The hero cannot change the Cosmos, but he can decide how he operates within it. He can change the culture, but not the nature of our world. The hero's task is to realign culture with nature and bring about the Golden Age.

Society needs heroes, but the hero is unassailable. He is, therefore, perpetually outside modern society due to his violent nature. Violence is what allows the warrior to survive and not succumb to the priestly class; it is the foundation of his power. A hero must be able to harness violence and use it when necessary.

The priest wants to supplant the warrior through guile and passive aggression. Their caste manipulates the warrior to its own ends, subverting him and the Tradition for which he stands. This is why he must always maintain the capacity for violence, or else be subjugated.

In epic, the hero is compared to a lion or another wild beast that attacks cattle. The hero is the predator attacking prey. Dog and wolf imagery is pervasive.

The dog, which man domesticated as a hunting and raiding companion, is assimilated by the warrior on the battlefield. He must be both man and beast. The canine symbolises that untameable part within man, representing the wild streak running through heroic society. The domesticated dog could devour society from within if it so chose.

To channel and control the inner beast is the ability of the true hero. He must not allow himself to be fully given over to the animal, but channel this wildness in a temporary state for a particular purpose: in order to affect change. This beast-like condition spells doom, however, if it cannot be undone. The hero's lower nature must never be allowed to fully give way to *lússā*: the rabid, berserk state. He must temper his impure animal side with the purity of honour.

At the summit of the hero's pure value system is honour. Honour above all – even his own life. Pure honour is personal integrity; the hero claims honour by performing honourable acts. He reaches beyond himself and promises himself greatness; he makes himself by assimilating himself. He goes into action to prove in action what he claims to be. The outcome is not certain, and here lies the honour.

The hero seeks purity and beauty in all his interactions. Ethics and aesthetics are not distinguished from each other. Inner purity and beauty are reflected outwardly. Spiritual and physical, social and personal: both are one and the same. Disorder on one level is reflected on all. When things are *en Kósmōi* (in order), order is pervasive. The hero must be vigilant, as his purity is constantly threatened by incursions.

A distinction can be made between young and mature heroes. The young hero is better suited to physical combat but lacks experience. Speech develops later in life and the young man's mind is hasty; his wits are slight. Age brings knowledge and authority; the mature hero is wiser, but his physical abilities are diminished. Battle and counsel are both arenas of excellence – the perfect hero is excellent in both speech and combat. He can control the mind which plans and the hand which executes.

Thought is the necessary complement of action, but they are also opposed. Deliberation can become inaction; being decisive, the hero must stop thinking at the correct juncture in order to act. He must rely on his forethought, then act in accordance with this while no longer contemplating.

Heroic Society

Heroic society has a preeminent warrior class that shares in responsibilities and renown. Heroic society is aristocratic; the chief works closely with his men, who are his equals. Like Agamemnon and his kings or King Arthur and the knights of the round table, the leader is "first among equals."

A class of men come to power through determination, cohesion, and clarity of purpose. They start as cattle raiders, youthful wolf warriors. The superior man in terms of will, courage, or intelligence becomes leader of the warband.

Individual prowess extends to the group, who are his equals in worth and honour. Glory is the ultimate goal in heroic society; by contributing to the group's glory, the hero gains his own. The glory and praise received by the hero in his lifetime and over his body at death are personal triumphs.

The band of heroes have solidarity in their shared purpose. They respect their chief, as he shares in their hardships and risks. They are proud of their superiority to other men and know they deserve special honour.

The heroes share a common sense of power. The Age of Heroes begins when heroic power is applied in a new direction with a new purpose. The difference between a warlike and heroic society is the value system of valour, honour, courage, and skilful action. The heroes channel Athena over Ares.

Heroic society escapes the perils of theocracy. Priestcraft and magic are one of the obstacles the band of heroes must overcome. Heroic pioneers bring the forces of priestcraft under control, assimilating them under the new set of conditions.

The Indian heroic age ended with the rise to power of the Brahmins. The priests mangled the heroic tales, turning them into sermons to their own ends. The priesthood never approved of the Heroic Tradition, but always unwittingly preserved its embers, seeking to use the tales to increase their power.

Heroic society also stands in stark contrast to the plutocracy of the merchants and kakistocracy of the mob, as neither of these groups respect or proliferate heroic values. Order has been turned on its head in the chaotic society of the modern world, and this must be reversed. Heroes must rise again, wresting power from institutions designed to oppress the heroic spirit.

The Hero and the Gods

The relationship between heroes and gods is subtle and complex; there is neither perfect alignment, nor pure opposition. The hero must work both with and against the gods in order to surpass them. All unfolds through the choices of both gods and men. Gods are defined by their powers and qualities, while heroes by their acts. Only heroes can recognise the gods in perfect clarity.

The ordering of the cosmos places man in a position of both great dignity and vulnerability. On the one hand, the regard of the gods gives heroes dignity – being loved by one or more of them allows the hero to achieve and ascend. Yet the gods are fickle, their allegiances temporary. Priam and the Trojans offer sacrifices to Zeus who loves them, but it does not stop Troy from being sacked.

The hero presses his advantage. The love of the gods is fleeting, so he cannot rely upon their graces. He must make his own way.

The gods do not watch over men, but simply watch them. Divine intervention is erratic, because the relationships between gods are unstable. The gods, through their detached use of men as pawns in their games, make themselves enemies of the hero.

The gods are frivolous, and their friendship or enmity have little to do with justice. They use the forces of nature, but do not guarantee the Cosmos. Their interventions are erratic and personal: they look out for their own interests. The hero strives against them while also serving their interests; he must make alliances with them in order to transcend them.

The gods, like men, are also restrained by nature. They did not create the Cosmos, but reside within it. The gods are not outside the world, but within it.

The gods are not epiphenomenal. They are a part of the phenomenal world, which they help shape but are also affected by. We contend with them in this cosmos. Only the hero can go beyond gods and nature. He achieves greatness and immortality in spite of them.

The gods envy heroes; but in this Age of Iron, they merely pity mankind. We must reverse that sentiment and live our lives in their fullest, most heroic manner. The power unleashed by the Age of Heroes is formidable, giving the individual honour at the expense of the gods and their agents who seek to hamper him.

The noise of battle reaches up to heaven – to fight the gods, one must do so indirectly and covertly. In the *Iliad* Diomedes says, "Do not strive to match the gods in battle." We must work against their wishes, while still honouring them in order to go beyond them.

The Coming Age of Heroes

The Age of Heroes fosters a whole generation equipped for war that finds satisfaction and reward in it. What survives for the modern hero is not necessarily the outer war, but the greater, inner, holy war. This inner holy war is the battle between Spirit and soul; it is the fight for the higher Self within the hero. This is reflected in the outer holy war against external foes. The transcended hero understands this outer fight to be a vehicle for his inner war.

Heroes are superior in physical strength, courage, endurance, control of their bodies, and willingness to sacrifice themselves for honour and fame. The emergence of the heroic spirit breaks through societal obstructions with determination and resourcefulness. It breeds an infectious confidence and thrives on victory and success. Nothing is impossible for men who have the courage and will to attempt what they want.

The individual emerges from the masses. He relies on his own strength and skill – his might. He is justified by his success.

Emancipation from the masses and bonds of cosmic restraint come only by way of effort and struggle. The Age of Heroes establishes the principle that men must rely on their own power. The hero relies on himself; he is aided by the divine and supernatural but determines his path and exerts his will.

The hero performs more than expected of him, rising up above his circumstances and lower nature, discharging forces lain dormant within him, unrecognised and unused. The hero must overcome both priestly, lunar spirituality and material, titanic virility. He must be a holy warrior, embodying true Olympian spirituality and masculine virility.

We have reached the bottom of the involution of the wheel of time. The new Age of Heroes is upon us. A reset is necessary to return to the Golden Age.

But this is only possible through the intervention of heroes – of men ready to act and do what is necessary in order for time to be reversed. Now is the time for our heroes to meet on the Cosmic battlefield to attain Undying Glory. It is time for us to find our way Home.

Part I: Origins

οἱ Μυκηναίοι

The Mykenaians

The epics of Homer and the Cyclic poets, as they have come down to us, are set against the backdrop of Mykenaian Greece. As we have established, the poems are layers built upon layers, extending back into a prehistoric, pre-Greek past. This has led to much scholarly discussion around the poems' historicity.

While they do not relate exact historical events from the Mykenaian period, it is worth having a look at this later Bronze Age layer of the epic story. The Greek Bronze Age (distinct from the Bronze Age in the Ages of Men cycle) spanned a 2000-year period from around 3200 BCE until the collapse of the Mykenaian palaces, circa 1200 BCE.

The Mykenaians were the first semi-urbanised Greeks. They were palace dwellers. The stories of heroes were sung in their palaces. They were, by then, part of the Mediterranean establishment. They were no longer of the caliber of the heroes of the epics.

The names of Mykenaian kings and princes were used in the songs, however. This is a new layer of a heroic period lain over ancient ones. The names of some kings and heroes in Homer may have been real, but their deeds were given a timelessness.

There has been much compelling archaeological evidence to suggest there was indeed a war waged on Troy by the Mykenaians. The excavations at Hissarlik (site of Troy) have yielded much to support some geographical and historical specifics mentioned by Homer. In conjunction with the translations of the Hittite tablets from the period, we can conclude there was likely a war of some description – and some names, like Agamemnon and Alexander (also known as Paris), were drawn from historical figures present at that time.

What we know of the Mykenaians is limited. They probably called themselves Akhaians, Danaans, and Argives as attested by Homer. Mykenaian was a name given them in the 19th century. They were a warlike Indo-European people who settled Greece from the north; and despite their palace building and semi-urbanisation, they retained this warrior aspect in their culture. The Linear B tablets show an aristocratic, militaristic, hierarchical society that was armed to the teeth with massive expenditure on war gear and palace ornamentation.

The tablets also show a distinct caste system was in place. At the top of the system were the warrior elite, property-owning priests, and craftsmen known in Mykenaian Greek as the *damos*.

Below these were the *teoio doero* – unnamed yet counted masses – the largest group in number. Much of the *dêmos* (masses) may have been non-Greek, Old European, Neolithic farmers. These were the people subjugated by the invading Indo-European people who became *āristoi* ("the best"): the ruling caste.

This warrior elite was geared for war and preoccupied with fighting and hunting. They used horses, chariots, and bronze weapons. To pay for weapons and regalia, Mykenaian kings went to war. These piratical raids for booty were necessary as commerce was not an option. The Mykenaians did not actively engage in large-scale trade, unlike the neighbouring Hittites, Egyptians, and Phoenicians; they were raiders instead.

Mykenaian kings sacked cities to gain booty, treasure, horses, cattle, gold, silver, armour, bronze, weapons, and women. The most coveted title they sought among their equals was "Sacker of Cities." They went to war with their aristocratic warband and regular army of untrained men from the *dêmos*.

We can gain more understanding of the Mykenaians by looking at the records of the Hittites of Asia Minor. The people we call Mykenaians were late-stage Akhaians. The Akhaians moved into Greece in 1800 BCE at the latest, but retained their Steppe culture for longer than the Hittites.

The Indo-European Hittites took over the territory of the non-Indo-European Hatti people in around 2000 BCE. They then adopted the urban, bureaucratic customs of the Akkadians and Babylonians. This included keeping extensive and detailed records on clay tablets.

The Hittite tablets indicate there was a "Great King" in Akhaia – likely Mykenai, likely of the Atreid dynasty (i.e. Agamemnon) – in the mid 1200s BCE. The Mykenaian word *wánax* (Ϝἄναξ) meaning "king of kings," "great king," or "over-king" describes this function.

A Hittite treaty from the 1200s names an Alaksandu of Wilusa, which translates to Alexandros (Paris) of Wilios (Ilios) in Mykenaian Greek. At this stage in history, Troy was a vassal state of the Hittite Empire, which was in terminal decline. Mykenai was at its peak between 1275-1260 BCE. By the time the Hittite documents about Wilusa and Alaksandu were written, the city of Ilios may well have been in Greek hands.

What is clear from the Hittite tablets is that the Akhaians caused major problems for the Hittites in the 13th century BCE, involving battles and skirmishes at which the Great King of the Akhaians was present. Likewise, the tale of the Trojan War is possibly based on a war between the Akhaian *wánax* (over-king), possibly called Agamemnon, and Troy (Ilios) in Western Anatolia next to the Dardanelles. The 10-year war of the Homeric record might paint a compressed picture of many Akhaian incursions into Anatolia and Northwest Asia Minor.

Another piece of evidence to add to this last layer of the heroic epic is that, while the Mykenaians mostly buried their dead, there is evidence of cremation at the supposed site of the Greek Camp on the ancient shoreline near the citadel of Troy.

The Mykenaian civilisation was broken up at its peak immediately following the timeframe for the Trojan War in the late 13th century BCE. This was due to several factors. Inter-house warfare between the nobles weakened the citadels, which were then attacked by the marauding "Sea Peoples," at least some of whom were Mykenaians themselves. This was followed by the "invasion" of the Dorian Greeks into the Peloponnese shortly after.

All kings are illegitimate in the beginning; it is only through the exercise of might they consummate their right to rule. The northern Dorians were also Greeks of Indo-European origin who moved into territory the Akhaians held and seized power, creating a new *āristoi*. This new nobility in the Peloponnese maintained some of the ancient citadels, performing rituals for the heroic cults that sprung up following the Mykenaian collapse. It was this new Dorian stock that would establish Sparta, the only remaining Greek kingdom in the Classical era with kings and a ruling warrior elite.

The Akhaians fled to Ionia (the coast of Asia Minor) taking their heroic epics with them. The tales sung by bards in the Mykenaian palaces were handed down by generations of Ionian rhapsodes who made their own poems based on the ancestral songs. The songs of the heroes of the last great battles of the Mykenaians were added as a layer to the great heroic epic story.

It is from this tradition the Homeric works have come to us.

ὁ κόσμος νοητός

The Perceptible Order

The ancient world of the Greeks and their ancestors was not constrained to the phenomenal world they saw with their eyes and experienced with their tangible senses. Instead, they experienced the universe as the *Kósmos noētós*: the "order perceptible to the mind." This included the higher reality that lay hidden beyond the world of phenomena.

Gaîa (Earth) is a great disk stretching out horizontally from the centre marked by the Omphalos stone at Delphoi, the navel of the Earth and manifested Axis Mundi. Surrounding the Earth disk is *Okeanós*, the Great Ocean. The vertical axis connects the Earth and *Kháos* (earth-bound air) with *Ólympos* (seat of the gods) and the *Aithêr* (heavenly bright air) enclosed by *Ouranós*, the solid dome of the sky. The axis also descends into *Aïdês* (the Underworld) and *Érebos* (murky mists of darkness). Below the Underworld is *Tártaros*, the deepest place in the cosmos, the place where disobedient gods are punished. Tartaros is as far beneath the Underworld as the heavens are above the Earth.

These places are all connected in the liminal spaces on the edge of Earth. Some groups of people, remnants of the Golden Age, live there, where the sky meets the earth on the shores of Okeanos. The Hyperborean, Aithiopian, and Phaiakian people exist on the edge of the Cosmos, entertaining the Olympians.

This liminal area at the edge of the earth is where *Ēlýsion pedíon* ("Elysian Fields"), *makárōn nêsoi* ("Isles of the Blessed"), *Leuké* ("White" Island), and the Garden of the Hesperides can be found. These paradise locations are where the heroes live after death, and where nymphs tend the sacred gardens of the gods.

The edges of the Earth also have entrances to the Underworld. The Gates of Helios, where the sun rises and sets, are on the shores of Okeanos. The sun intersects the vertical and the horizontal dimensions.

The sun rises from the Underworld each morning and returns there each night. He carries the souls of men to death as he sets and resurrects the dead when he rises. These gates are the region of dreams.

Rather than being polar opposites – as in the Abrahamic religions – the Underworld and paradise locations exist on a continuum. These worlds can also be touched by mortal men. It is in these liminal places that divinities and supernatural beings interact with human heroes.

The edge of the Earth has a temporal as well as spacial conflation. The past, present, and future mix there. This is how Kronos can still oversee the Golden Age on the Isles of the Blessed. The Plain of Elysion, Leuke, and the Isles of the Blessed are all manifestations of the heroic paradise, somewhat similar to the Germanic Valhalla. This is an Indo-European inheritance.

Life there is easy, with good weather and plentiful crops. The inhabitants stay animated, unlike the shades of the general dead in the Underworld. It is a horizontal paradise on the same material plane as the Earth, on the shores of the great world-encircling river Okeanos. It is located where the sun rises and sets on the border of the Underworld.

This is home of the *héroes hagnoí* ("holy heroes") who, in return for having their life cut short in battle, receive a state of immortality on the liminal edges of the cosmos between the human and divine worlds. The hero who turns fire into light exists there in an ethereal body, wandering through fields of light in the immaterial lands of blessed heroes.

All Ages exist at the same time and at no time. Aithiopians, Hyperboreans, and Phaiakians are parallel to the race of men in the Golden Age. They live on the edge of the cosmos, where time does not exist.

The Aithiopians live at both the places of sunrise and sunset, split between the two. The Hyperboreans live in the far North, the True North. The Phiakians are in the South and act as the ferrymen for the dead, bringing the ritually dead heroes back to the land of the living.

By unifying the mind, the hero can obtain the Olympian Stare that destroys the veil covering the universe. This is the divine gaze given temporarily to Diomedes in order to send the gods running back to Olympos. With this vision, all of the perceptible order is laid bare. This is a metaphor for the process whereby the hero achieves a higher level of perception.

The hero is able to travel as he wishes between worlds, opening the fastened doorways of the four directions. Having seeing knowledge of the gods, he has power over them. He is able to free himself of their bonds, going beyond to the great Polar Centre where he can see all unfold before him.

ὁ Ἐπικὸς Κύκλος

The Epic Cycle

The works of Homer once had their place in what was referred to in antiquity as the Epic Cycle. This group of epic poems translated the entire heroic mythology of the Greeks into lyric form. The first attested use of the term "Epic Cycle" appears in Aristotle, but is used to refer to the works that survived into the Hellenistic period. The scholars at the Library of Alexandria heavily edited these works to make a singular narrative that fit the works of Homer, which they thought to be superior.

While scholars have debated which came first (the Cyclic poems or the Homeric), the original epics have been chanted from before the Greeks were Greek. They are ancient Indo-European tales passed down through the generations with new names and deeds overlaid on the timeless mythos. All the Epic Cycle poems are based in these earlier oral roots, as are the *Iliad* and *Odyssey*.

Oral mythical traditions do not require manifestation in image or text to exist and be well-known. To pin a date of composition on them is pointless. They all come down to us from the Indo-European hero mythos. The academic debate raging over which poems were earlier and influenced the later is of no interest; all Cyclic poems are equally true when viewed from a mythic standpoint.

The stories of the Epic Cycle are derived from the mythological record – from stories already known to the Greek people. They are the Indo-European myths given a Bronze Age historical setting for people with an increasing awareness of their Greek identity. In other words, Greek mythology was already well-formed before the Homeric poems.

The story told in the Epic Cycle was known and understood by the Greeks. The Homeric poems, for example, assume the listener already knows the events of the Trojan War. The individual poems focussed on different parts of the story known to the audience. There were even more epic poems lost entirely by the Hellenistic period. Thousands of poets sang of the Trojan War, of the creation of the gods, of older heroes and generations of men.

The Cyclic poems existed orally, independent of each other, along with innumerable epic poems. They were continually recreated until they were solidified and committed to paper in the Archaic Period. Epics regarding Herakles (such as the *Oikhalias Halosis*) are lost entirely, but we know they existed through fragments in later writers.

The Epic Cycle is a manifestation of the mythological past, collected and recorded as a literate substitution for traditions that were dying out in the Hellenistic Era. The Alexandrian scholars attempted to preserve and make palatable these poems, which contained what was considered vulgar by their time. What remained in existence was the *Titanomakhia* (War of the Titans) and two cycles: the Theban Cycle and the Trojan Cycle. Both of these together were part of the most recent Age of Heroes to the Greeks. They added deeds of Akhaians and Trojans to the heroic current: the timeless, powerful, and true tradition of the Indo-European people.

The Cyclic style was faster paced than the Homeric. The poems employed magic, oracles, and immortality more than Homer did. These more folkish beliefs are mostly rejected in his work.

None of his heroes are explicitly immortal or invulnerable, whereas they were in the other works of the Epic Cycle. This immortality and invulnerability would diminish their valour in the Homeric tellings. Homer also glosses over less palatable parts of tales the other epics embrace, such as the incestuous relationship of Oidipous and Iokaste.

The Cyclic poems were a more direct representation of the Cyclic myth. The Homeric were considered more sophisticated renderings by the Hellenistic scholars. The *Iliad* and *Odyssey* are often classified as "metacyclic;" while similar to the Cyclic poems, they are closer in style and content to each other.

They are probably related, but were not likely composed by a single poet. Homer may not have been an actual person, and the *Iliad* and *Odyssey* may or may not have been composed by the same hand. However, this book sticks to tradition for convenience's sake, attributing both to Homer.

The Cyclic poems all drew from the same mythic tradition, and each poem had its place in it. They did not influence each other directly before they were edited in the Hellenistic period. That they were extensively copied – and survive to this day – is due to the fact Homeric works were considered superior by Hellenistic standards.

The Cyclic poems were no less valid than the Homeric; they were not inferior, but were devalued over time. It was in the Hellenistic period they became scorned in favour of Homeric poems. Beginnings and endings of poems were cut by Alexandrian scholars to make them fit together. The *Kypria* and the *Aithiopis*, which bookend the Iliad, were heavily edited to fit the Homeric narrative. The *Ilias Mikra* was severely cut to slot it into a place in a continuous narrative.

The Homeric Work was more palatable to the post-Hellenic world that derided some of the folkloric and magical elements in the other Cyclic poems. Archaic beliefs were disdained, and

Homer's works were probably purged of distasteful material, although the *Odyssey* retains more than the Iliad.

The *Odyssey* tells the tale of Odysseus – a popular figure after the Trojan War – and has a clear place in the cycle. The *Iliad*, however, emphasises a very brief period of the war that other poems of the Epic Cycle may have glossed over. Homeric poetry widened the roles and characters of certain heroes, providing a more expansive version of traditional myth. These works were also Pan-Hellenic, while the other poems emphasised the roles of heroes from the city-states that commissioned their commitment to paper. The *Kypria* emphasised Miletos, and the *Telegony* did the same for Kyrene.

The other poems of the Cycle were lost over time, but through the fragments it is possible to reconstruct the plot in its entirety. Mined extensively by tragedians like Sophokles and Aischylos as plot material and quoted in the works of later writers, enough of the tales survive for some literary forensics.

Using the summaries left by Proklos (which records the events of the Trojan Cycle in its final edited stage), and supplementing it with Pindaros, Apollodoros, Pausanias, Apollonios Rhodios, and Quintus of Smyrna – as well as the scholia (notes in the margins of ancient manuscripts) and clues in the *Iliad* and *Odyssey* – a little literary detective work yields an incredible tale of several generations of gods and heroes.

The poet is a seer: a channel of ancestral memory. The editor is an academic, concerned with making things fit into their worldview. That being established, let us take a look at what has survived and step back from the nit-picking to gain a fuller view of the mythos presented by the Epic Cycle.

The following summaries tell the story in its totality. Some of the epics have more extant fragments than the others, so there are more details. The main surviving fragment of each is italicised at the beginning of each summary. As the ancients understood the *Iliad* and the *Odyssey* in their full context, these summaries place them in this context once more.

ἡ Τιτανομαχία

The *Titanomakhia*

"In the midst of them danced the Father of men and gods."

Ouranos (Father Sky) lays with Gaia (Mother Earth) fathering the three giant Hekatonkheires (Hundred-Handers): Briareos, Gyes and Kottos. He next sires the three Kyklopes: Arges, Steropes, and Brontes. Seeing the mighty power of his offspring, Ouranos binds them and casts them into Tartaros, the deepest part of the Underworld – as far below Gaia as Ouranos is above her. He next fathers the Titans (Okeanos, Koios, Hyperion, Kreios, Iapelos, and Kronos) and the Titanesses (Tethys, Rhea, Themis, Memnosyne, Phoibe, Doine, and Theia).

Gaia grows angry at the loss of her first children and asks the Titans to attack Ouranos, giving Kronos the Harpe (an adamantine sickle). Aside from Okeanos, they all assault their father. Kronos, the youngest, cuts off Ouranos' genitals and throws them into the sea. Three drops of blood fall to the Earth, becoming the Erinyes (Furies): Alekto, Tisiphone, and Megaira.

The Titans bring their giant brothers up from Tartaros and enthrone Kronos. The new ruler of the Cosmos sends the Hundred-Handers and Kyklopes back to Tartaros, as he fears their immense power. He then marries his sister Rhea.

Ouranos and Gaia prophecy that Kronos will be deposed by his own child. Each time Rhea bears offspring, he swallows them to prevent this. The gods born to Kronos and Rhea are Hestia, Demeter, Hades, and Poseidon.

When Rhea is pregnant with Zeus, she goes to Krete and gives birth to him in a cave on Mount Dikte. She gives him to the nymphs and Kouretes to raise. Rhea then wraps a stone in swaddling and gives it to Kronos, who swallows it, believing it to be the infant.

Zeus grows up, and with the help of Metis (daughter of Okeanos) he administers an emetic to Kronos. The Titan vomits up Zeus' older siblings. The gods wage war on the Titans from Mount Olympos, attacking the older gods on their home of Mount Orthros. After ten years, Gaia tells Zeus he can only win if he frees the Hundred-Handers and Kyklopes. Zeus kills Kampe, jailer of the ancient beings, releasing them.

The Kyklopes forge the Thunderbolt for Zeus, the Helm of Darkness for Hades, and the Trident for Poseidon. Using these weapons, the Olympians defeat the Titans, casting them into

Tartaros. The Hundred-Handers are charged with guarding them. Kronos and Rhea are sent to the Isles of the Blessed.

The Olympians then cast lots for dominion. Zeus takes power over the sky, Poseidon the sea, and Hades the Underworld. Zeus marries his sister Hera and sires Hephaistos and Ares. Aphrodite is born from the genitals of Ouranos that were thrown into the sea. Zeus also sires Apollon and Artemis with Leto, as well as Hermes with Maia.

The king of the gods impregnates Metis, but then discovers from Gaia that the son who may follow the daughter from this union with her will become the ruler of heaven. He swallows Metis and then gives birth to Athena from his head. The goddess emerges in full battle dress shouting a piercing war cry.

Prometheus creates the race of men. However, he pities them and steals fire from the gods to help them. Zeus punishes him by chaining him to Mount Kaukasos in Skythia.

Angry with the Olympians over the fate of the Titans, Gaia produces the Giants with Ouranos. The greatest of these are Porphyrion and Alkyoneus. It is prophesied that the gods need the aid of a mortal to defeat the Giants, so they enlist the help of Herakles.

The hero and the gods kill the Giants. The Titan Atlas is tasked with holding up the heavens, separating Gaia from

Ouranos. Gaia becomes even more enraged and copulates with Tartaros itself, bearing the monster Typhon. A mix of man and dragon, he is the largest of all of Gaia's offspring.

The gods flee Olympos at the sight of him, but Zeus stands his ground. Typhon cuts out Zeus' sinews, hiding them and placing the immobile Zeus in the Korykian Cave. Hermes and Aigipan steal the sinews, restoring them to Zeus.

Mounting his chariot, Zeus fights Typhon. He drives the dragon back using his Thunderbolts. Then Zeus buries Typhon under Mount Etna.

ὁ Θηβαϊκὸς Κύκλος

The Theban Cycle

The Theban cycle is made up of four epics: the *Oidpodeia*, *Thebais*, *Epigonoi*, and *Alkmaionis*. Very little survives of the cycle, but we can reconstruct the narrative and gain insight into its heroes.

Oidipous is a tragic hero and son of Laios, whose wickedness begins a cycle of death and retribution. The acts of Oidipous resonate through the lives of his sons Polyneikes and Eteokles, who fight over the rulership of Thebes after Oidipous' death.

Polyneikes and his allies, collectively known as "the Seven," are warlike heroes filled with fury, rage, pride, brutality, and bloodlust. They are titanic in their behaviours and appetites. Like Herakles, they are rougher heroes of an earlier age who are eventually supplanted by more Olympian heroes.

Polyneikes is a cunning rogue. Kapaneus is an arrogant blasphemer struck down by Zeus. The most famous of them is Tydeus, father of Diomedes.

Sired by Oineus and his war bride Periboea, Tydeus is a brutal bully, but a favourite of the goddess Athena. He is small in physical stature, but a blood-thirsty and violent warrior. Tydeus' character is of high and crude antiquity.

He has great strength and performs heroic feats, but meets an evil fate. He has a violent temper and performs hasty, unconsidered actions. Tydeus is capable of both valiant and cruel deeds – a knight errant with a piratical Mykenaian nature.

The unsuccessful attack by the Seven on the city of Thebes is avenged by their sons, the Epigonoi. Of these, Diomedes, son of Tydeus, is best known. He is the young boar, greedy for action and ready to send the gods running from his spear. He is more refined than his father Tydeus, but has inherited some of his titanic nature. Both Diomedes and his fellow Epigonos, Sthenelos, fight with the Akhaians at Troy.

The Theban Cycle sets the stage for the Trojan Cycle. It tells the stories of the older generation of heroes, and circumstances leading to the relational inheritance of the heroes of Troy. It traces the lineage of the heroes from the gods, setting in place feuds and power dynamics present in the Trojan material.

ἡ Οἰδιπόδεια

The *Oidipodeia*

"But by far the fairest and most desirable of them all, the dear son of blameless Kreon, noble Haimon, [the Sphynx destroyed]."

Hera, the queen of the gods, sends the monstrous Sphynx to Thebes to punish the Thebans for the homosexuality of the king Laios. Laios had abducted the handsome youth Khrysippos and raped him. The boy committed suicide out of shame, prompting Hera to punish the city.

An oracle – possibly that of Delphoi – tells Laios that if he has a son, the boy will kill him and marry his own mother. Laios' wife Iokaste (called Euryganeia in the Oidipodeia) bears him a son.

The baby's heels are pierced with pins and he is exposed on Mount Kithairon. He is then rescued by a shepherd and given to Polybos and Merope (or Periboia), the king and queen of Korinth.

The boy is named Oidipous (Swollen Feet) due to his injury. As a youth, he travels to Delphoi and learns from the oracle that he is fated to kill his own father and marry his mother. Oidipous does not return to Korinth, unaware of his true parentage.

He instead travels to Thebes, but while passing Mount Kithairon, he encounters a traveller who demands he move aside. This argument breaks out in violence. Oidipous kills the man, not knowing that he is Laios, his true father.

He arrives in Thebes and discovers that the king of the city is recently dead, and that the Sphynx has the city locked in terror. The regent, Haimon, son of Kreon (brother of Iokaste), has also been killed by the Sphynx. Since there is no young man to rule the city, Kreon has declared that whoever defeats the sphynx will marry Iokaste and become the new king.

The Sphynx has the head of a woman, body of a lion, and wings of a bird. She has learned a riddle from the muses, and will devour young people from the city every day until someone is able to answer the question. The riddle is: "What is four-footed and two-footed and three-footed though it has but one voice?"

The answer is man. This is because he crawls as an infant, walks upright as an adult, and uses a walking stick as an old man. Oidipous answers the riddle of the Sphynx, and the monster throws itself to its death.

Not knowing that she is his own mother, Oidipous marries Iokaste and sires four children with her. He then discovers the truth. Iokaste hangs herself; Oidipous tears out his own eyes, but continues to rule Thebes.

ἡ Θηβαΐς

The *Thebais*

"Of Argos sing, goddess, the thirsty city from which the lords [of the expedition against Thebes set forth]…"

Oidipous curses his sons Polyneikes and Eteokles for an indiscretion. Either they place before him the table and cup of his father Laios (reminding him of his patricide), or give him the haunch rather than the shoulder from a sacrificial animal (a less honourable portion). The curse of Oidipous says that the two will not divide their patrimony on friendly terms, and that they will go to war with each other.

Polyneikes, the elder, but sinister brother is the one who places the forbidden cup before Oidipous. Alternatively, he is the one who sends the haunch to the blind old king (who has given sacrificial duties over to his sons).

Oidipous dies and Polyneikes leaves Thebes, or is expelled by Eteokles. Before he leaves, he takes some of the treasure from the Theban storeroom, including the cursed necklace and "peplos" (dress) of Harmonia, the wife of Kadmos who founded the city. He takes what he needs in order to make trouble against Thebes.

At the same time, the hero Tydeus is exiled from Kalydon by his uncle Agrios for killing his other uncle Alkathoös or some of his cousins (the sons of Melas). Both Polyneikes and Tydeus arrive in Argos; they meet outside the palace of King Adrastos and get into a conflict with each other. Tydeus wears the hide of a boar and Polyneikes the pelt of a lion. As they begin to battle, Adrastos remembers a prophecy that told him to yoke his daughters in marriage to these two animals. Tydeus is married to Deipyle and Polyneikes to Argeia.

Adrastos then rashly promises to restore both men to their native lands. Polyneikes and Tydeus set about assembling chieftains for an expedition against Thebes, even though the gods are hostile to this assault. They gather five more heroes: Kapaneus, Eteoklos, Hippomedon, Parthenopaios, and Amphiaraos.

The last, Amphiaraos, is betrayed by his wife, Eriphyle, into joining the battle. She is bribed by Polyneikes with the necklace of Harmonia in order to compel her husband. After becoming oath-bound, he has no choice other than fight.

As a seer, Amphiaraos envisions his own death. He tells his son Alkmaion to avenge him and attack Thebes once he is of age.

These proud and brutal Seven, led by King Adrastos, begin their journey to seven-gated Thebes.

Their journey takes them through Nemea. Here they meet the exiled queen of Lemnos, Hypsipyle, nursing the infant prince of Nemea, Opheltes. The infant is killed by a serpent that is in turn killed by the Seven. They then compete in funeral games for the prince, which are the foundation of the later Nemean Games. As they leave, one of the Seven renames the infant Archemoros, meaning "Beginning of Doom," as his death is an ill omen.

The Seven arrive at Mount Kithairon and send Tydeus ahead to tell Eteokles to yield. This entreaty is rejected and Tydeus challenges the Thebans to athletic contests, beating all with Athena's help. The angry Thebans set an ambush for him, but Tydeus kills his assailants, sparing only Maion (son of Haimon) and sending him back to Thebes.

At first, the Argives win a preliminary victory over the Thebans at the river Ismenos. The Thebans are driven back to their city and the Seven lay siege. Each commander is assigned one of the seven gates of Thebes to assault.

The Thebans consult their seer Teiresias. He tells them they will be successful if Menoikeus, son of Kreon, sacrifices himself to Ares. Without hesitation, Menoikeus cuts his own throat at the gates of Thebes.

Kapaneus attempts to scale the wall of Thebes and is blasted down with a thunderbolt by Zeus for his pride. This causes a retreat of the Argive forces, and the Thebans sally forth to slaughter them. Eteokles and Polyneikes duel and kill each other. Hippomedon is killed by Ismaros, Eteoklos by Leades, and Parthenopaios by Amphidikos.

Tydeus is mortally wounded by Melanippos, who is then killed by Amphiaraos. The seer perceives Athena is about to give Tydeus a potion that will make him immortal. As Amphiaraos is hostile to Tydeus for bringing him into the battle, he brings the head of Melanippos to Tydeus.

Tydeus gnaws on Melanippos' brains. This disgusts his patroness Athena, who denies her favourite the immortality she was about to bestow upon him. Tydeus realises this and asks that she give it to his son Diomedes instead.

Amphiaraos rides away from the battle on his four-horse chariot. However, he is swallowed by the Earth after Zeus opens it with a Thunderbolt. As a seer, Amphiaraos' place after death is under Earth: a burial, not a cremation.

King Adrastos survives and rides back to Argos on his divine horse Arion. He has a funeral for the Seven. Kapaneus' wife throws herself onto her husband's funeral pyre.

οἱ Ἐπίγονοι

The *Epigonoi*

"And now, Muses, let us begin to sing of younger men."

Ten years later, the seven sons of the original Seven successfully lay siege to Thebes. Led by Adrastos' son Aigialeus, they sack the city, avenging their fathers.

These *"Epigonoi"* (Progeny) are Thersander, Diomedes, Alkmaion, Amphilochos, Euryalos, Sthenelos, and Promachos. When the Epigonoi assault Thebes, Teiresias tells the Thebans to send a herald out to the Argives while the rest escape the city.

The Thebans flee. Teiresias drinks from the Tilphoussa Spring and dies. His shade descends to the Asphodel Meadows in the Underworld.

The Argives plunder Thebes and take down the walls. They send to Delphoi a portion of the booty, including Manto, daughter of Teiresias.

Sacrifice, according to the interpretation of the fragments and the ancient commentaries, is a powerful motif in the epic, but very little survives. This thematic device is not fully understandable now based on the scant fragmentary excerpts that survive.

ἡ Ἀλκμαιωνίς

The *Alkmaionis*

"And stretching the corpses on a broad couch spread on the ground, he set before them a rich feast, and cups, and he placed garlands on their heads."

Likely covering much of what is in the *Epigonoi*, the *Alkmaionis* tells the story of Alkmaion, son of Amphiaraos. He too learns he is betrayed by his mother Eriphyle, and kills her in an act of vengeance as instructed by Apollon.

After the death of Tydeus, the sons of his uncle Agrios depose his father Oineus and imprison him. Diomedes, along with Alkmaion, arrive from Argos and slay the sons of Agrios, placing Andraimon (Oineus' son-in-law) on the throne. Two of the sons, Thersites and Onechestos, escape and kill Oineus. Diomedes takes the corpse to Argos for a funeral before heading to Troy.

While Diomedes is in Aitolia dispatching the sons of Agrios, Agamemnon establishes his rule in Argos. When Diomedes returns, Agamemnon relinquishes power to him, but obliges him to participate in the Trojan War.

The *Alkmaionis* also relates the story of brothers Telamon and Peleus, fathers of Aias and Akhilleus. Telamon and Peleus kill their half-brother Phokos. Telemon throws a diskos at him, then Peleus strikes him with an axe.

Their father, King Aikos, banishes them from Aigina. Telamon goes to Salamis and Peleus to Phthia. The two brothers are both Argonauts, and join Herakles on his expedition against the Amazons.

Part II: Troy

ὁ Τρωϊκός Κύκλος

The Trojan Cycle

The Trojan Cycle is made up of eight epics: the *Kypria*, *Iliad*, *Aithiopis*, *Ilias Mikra* ("Little Iliad"), *Iliou Persis* (Sack of Troy), *Nostoi* (Returns), *Odyssey*, and *Telegony*. More survives of this cycle than the Theban, but most were cut down to fit the narratives of the *Iliad* and *Odyssey* even before they were lost.

The story starts with the decision of Zeus to reduce the burden of the earth, along with the marriage of Peleus and Thetis, parents of Akhilleus. It narrates the story of the circumstances that start the Trojan War, and gathering of the heroes by Agamemnon, king of Mykenai.

Aside from Akhilleus and Odysseus (both of whom will be discussed in detail later in this book), other heroes come to the fore in these poems. Diomedes ravages the Trojans and goes on missions with his comrade Odysseus. Akhilleus' cousin Aias, son of Telemon, gains great glory on the battlefield, but eventually meets a cruel fate.

Aias butchers the cattle of the Akhaians, violating the code of slaughter out of madness and despair at his loss of *aristeíā* (prestige) to Odysseus. Everything he has done at Troy is meaningless to him unless he is considered best.

Neoptolemos, son of Akhilleus, and Philoktetes come to Troy and push the fight in favour of the Akhaians. The city is sacked through the device of the wooden horse. The Akhaians anger the gods and very few make it home. Agamemnon returns home after the sack of Troy to be slaughtered by his brother and his own wife.

Menelaos returns after years at sea. Diomedes is exiled upon his return. Nestor returns home safely, but without his son Antilokhos, who is fated to die at Troy.

The Trojans and their allies have their share of heroes too. The war at Troy does not set heroes against villains, but hero against hero. They are neither wholly good nor bad. Hektor, Paris, Sarpedon, Eurypylos, and Memnon all have moments of glory before meeting their violent ends.

The Trojan Cycle marks the end of the last Age of Heroes. Although its reverberation can still be felt today. With the rise of the age of urbanisation, however, the role of the hero has become corrupted.

τά Κύπρια

The *Kypria*

"There was a time when the countless tribes of men, though wide-dispersed, oppressed the surface of the deep-bosomed earth, and Zeus saw it and had pity and in his wise heart resolved to relieve the all-nurturing earth of men by causing the great struggle of the Ilian war, that the load of death might empty the world. And so the heroes were slain in Troy, and the plan of Zeus came to pass."

Zeus decides to instigate the Trojan War to lighten the load on Earth, which is straining under the sheer number of men. He plans this with the goddess Themis (Council).

In the Kypria, Nemesis is the mother of Helen and Zeus is the father. They pair as geese and Helen is born from an egg. Nemesis is a parallel to Themis and the righteous war will be fought over her daughter. Leda, queen of Sparta, finds the egg and nurtures the child.

Themis resolves a rivalry between Zeus and Poseidon over the sea goddess, Thetis, by prophesying the son of Themis will be mightier than his father. She discovers this from the Titan Prometheus. The son, if a god, will be ruler of the Universe.

Zeus makes an oath that the nymph Thetis will marry a mortal, and Hera rewards Thetis for resisting Zeus' advances. Hera raised Thetis, so she is loyal to the mother goddess. Thetis, who is the daughter of Nereus, marries Peleus. Encouraged by the centaur Kheiron, Peleus wrestles Thetis in order to get her. The sea-sprite changes shape continuously until finally submitting.

Peleus sacks Iolkos, then returns to Phthia to celebrate his marriage. This takes place on Mount Pelion and all the gods gather to feast, giving Peleus and Thetis gifts. Kheiron gives Peleus an ashen spear polished by Athena with a point fitted by Hephaistos. This is the spear that both Peleus and his son Akhilleus carry in battle. Dionysos gives Thetis a golden amphora, which will one day house the remains of Akhilleus in his tumulus. Poseidon gives Peleus the immortal horses Xanthos and Balios.

Eris (Strife) was not invited to the wedding and, therefore, omitted from the sacrificial honours. She causes an argument about beauty between Athena, Hera, and Aphrodite, throwing a golden apple to the ground "for the fairest."

Hermes leads the goddesses to the shepherd Paris on Mount Ida to adjudicate. Paris chooses Aphrodite after she promises him union with Helen. This sets Athena and Hera against the Trojans.

Akhilleus is child of the union of Peleus and Thetis. Thetis attempts to burn away Akhilleus' mortal part on a fire each night, but is caught in the act by Peleus who has no understanding. The goddess abandons both father and child.

Peleus hands the boy over to the centaur Kheiron to raise. Akhilleus is fed on a diet of the raw innards of lions and the living marrow of boars, bears, and wolves. Through this, he takes on their strength, speed, and agility.

All of this is set in motion by Zeus' council with Themis.

Hekube, queen of Troy, dreams she is pregnant with a fire brand that burns down Troy. When Paris is born, Priam (king of Troy) gives the infant to the shepherd Agelaos to kill. The shepherd raises the boy instead.

Paris returns to Troy after judging the goddesses, where he is immediately recognised. Aphrodite instructs Paris to build ships. She commands her son Aineias to sail with him. First Helenos, then Kassandra (both children of Priam) deliver doom-laden prophesies regarding the future. Paris and Aineias sail to Sparta.

Paris is first entertained in Lakadaimonia by the semi-divine Dioskouri – twin brothers of Helen. Kastor is son of King Tyndareus, while his brother Polydeukes is son of Zeus. At the banquet, the cousins of the Dioskouri (the Apharetidai twins Idas and Lynkeus) insult them.

A long-standing feud boils over regarding the brides of the Dioskouri, who were originally betrothed to the Apharetidai. The Apharetidai mock the Dioskouri for failing to give bridal gifts to Leukippos, father of their brides. The Dioskouri threaten to perform a cattle raid on the herds of Aphareus (their cousins' father), and give them to their father-in-law. This quarrel was also devised by Zeus.

The Trojans are then feasted for nine days by Menelaos in Sparta, and Paris gives gifts to Helen. Menelaos then has to depart to Krete for his grandfather Katreus' funeral. He instructs Helen to entertain his guests.

Helen and Paris join in union, setting sail for Troy in the middle of the night. They likewise steal a horde from the palace treasury. The Palladion statue of Athena could have been part of this treasure.

Helen abandons her daughter Hermione. Hera sends a storm, forcing the Trojan ships to land in Sidon. Paris sacks the city before sailing to Troy where the pair marry.

In the meantime, the Dioskouri raid the cattle of Aphareus as promised. Lynkeus spots the twins hiding in a hollow oak tree and sneaks up on them, killing Kastor. Polydeukes then kills Idas and Lynkeus. Zeus confers alternating immortality to the Dioskouri at the request of Polydeukes.

Iris reports the abduction to Menelaos, who goes to consult his brother Agamemnon regarding an expedition against Troy. The pair then visit Nestor, and the three kings travel through Greece gathering chieftains. The "Oath of Tyndareus" is invoked in order to gather the Greek forces.

When the kings of Greece were courting Helen, they made an oath that they would defend the rights of the successful suitor. The oath was suggested to Tyndareus by Odysseus when the king worried that fighting would break out regarding his decision as to who would marry his daughter. In return, Odysseus was awarded Penelope, niece of Tyndareus.

When Menelaos arrives on Ithake, Odysseus puts on a pretence of insanity to avoid war, as he is not oathed; but Palamedes snatches his son Telemakhos and threatens to kill him, forcing Odysseus to admit his sanity and join. Another possible story is that Odysseus – as part of his pretence – yokes an ass and ox to a plough, sowing salt instead of seed. In this iteration, Palamedes places Telemakhos in the path of the plough in order to reveal Odysseus' sanity.

Thetis hides Akhilleus among the girls at Skyros at age nine, after the seer Kalkhas predicts Troy cannot fall without him. When he comes of age he sires Neoptolemos with Deidaneia, daughter of King Lykomedes. The Greek Chieftains arrive at Skyros and Odysseus detects Akhilleus by placing weapons before the girls. These are picked up by Akhilleus, who cannot resist them. Knowing that his destiny is to either live long with no glory, or die young at Troy with Undying Glory, he chooses the latter.

The chieftains assemble at Aulis and sacrifice to Apollon. During the ritual, the Greeks see a serpent devour nine sparrow chicks and their mother, after which Zeus turns the snake to stone as a monument for all time. The seer Kalkhas interprets this to mean the Greeks will take Troy in the tenth year.

The Greeks then land in Mysia and lay siege to the city of Tithrania, when they are stopped from disembarking by the watchmen. A day of battle ensues. The king Telephos, son of Herakles, defends his realm, killing Thersander, son of Polyneikes of Thebes. Telephos is then wounded by Akhilleus and the Greeks set sail. The fleet is scattered by a storm and Akhilleus puts in at Skyros.

The wounded Telephos later arrives at Argos as instructed by an oracle. Akhilleus, who is there with the other Greeks, heals him. In return, Telephos tells the Akhaians the way to Troy.

After further preparations, the Akhaian fleet is once again assembled at Aulis. Agamemnon kills a deer while hunting and boasts that his shot with an arrow is better than that of Artemis. In retaliation, the goddess traps the fleet in the harbour.

Under the instruction of Kalkhas, the Greeks are told they have to sacrifice Agamemnon's daughter Iphigenia in order to leave. Agamemnon summons the girl under pretence of marriage to Akhilleus. When they attempt to sacrifice her, Artemis snatches the girl away to be her immortal priestess among the Taurians, substituting her with a sacrificial deer.

The fleet sail to Tenedos, laying siege to the island. In the melee Akhilleus kills King Tenes. He does so despite a warning from his mother this will doom him to be slain by Apollon.

On Tenedos, the hero Philoktetes is bitten by a water snake. This leaves him with a stinking, festering wound. The Greeks decide to abandon him on the island of Lemnos.

The Greeks disembark at Troy and immediately battle with the Trojans. Protosilaos is first off the ships and, after killing many Trojans, is slain by Hektor. Akhilleus' mother Thetis warned him not to be the first to disembark, as it was the fate of that hero to be first killed. Akhilleus puts the Trojans into flight by slaying Poseidon's son Kyknos with a rock.

The Greeks recover their dead. They send an embassy to Troy with Odysseus and Menelaos to demand the return of Helen and the treasure. This demand is denied by the Trojans, so the Greeks build their defensive wall and ravage the surrounding towns and countryside.

Akhilleus wishes to see Helen, so Thetis and Aphrodite secretly bring them together and they join in sexual union. A number of Greeks want to return home, but Akhilleus convinces them to stay. Odysseus takes revenge on Palamedes for embroiling him in the war, drowning him with the help of Diomedes.

Akhilleus drives away the cattle of Aineias during a raid and sacks the towns of Pedasos and Lyrnessos. He then ambushes and kills the child prince Troilos at the temple of Thymbrian Apollon. He does this despite the warning from Thetis not to do so, thereby invoking the further wrath of Apollon.

Patroklos captures Lykaon and sells him into slavery at Lemnos. Aias and Akhilleus sack many cities allied to Troy. From the spoils, Akhilleus takes the girl Briseis, and Agamemnon takes Kryseis.

After nine years of siege, the Trojan allies begin to arrive.

ἡ Ἰλιάς

The *Iliad*

"Rage-Goddess, sing the rage of Peleus' son Akhilleus"

After a terrible plague ravages the Akhaians, Agamemnon is forced to return Kryseis to her father to appease Apollon. Spitefully, he takes Briseis from Akhilleus, who has petitioned him the hardest about the return of Kryseis. The hero is angered to the point of wishing to attack Agamemnon, but instead withdraws from the battle.

The Trojans take the fight to the Greeks. Paris fights Menelaos, but is rescued by Aphrodite when he is about to lose. Diomedes dominates the battlefield, wounding both Aphrodite and Ares and sending them back to Olympos. Hektor duels Aias, but the fight ends with a stalemate due to nightfall.

The Trojans drive the Greeks back behind their defensive wall. The Greeks send an embassy to Akhilleus, but he rejects their pleas. The Trojans break through the Akhaian defences and burn some of their ships.

Akhilleus sends Patroklos out to fight dressed in his armour. The Trojans flee and many are cut down. But Patroklos is killed by Hektor, who takes Akhilleus' armour from him. His body is fought for, and eventually taken back to the Greek camp.

Filled with grief for his friend, Akhilleus sets aside his anger. He accepts the gifts of Agamemnon and his return of Briseis. In order that he can go into battle and kill Hektor, he reconciles with Agamemnon.

Akhilleus is rearmed by the god Hephaistos. He routs the Trojans before dueling Hektor outside the city walls of Troy, where he has been trapped by Athena. After a hard fight, Akhilleus kills Hektor and mutilates his body.

Funeral games are held for Patroklos. Priam visits Akhilleus and pays ransom for Hektor's body, bringing it back to Troy for a funeral.

τό Αἰθιοπίς

The *Aithiopis*

"Then came the Amazon, the daughter of great-souled Ares the slayer of men."

The Amazon Penthesileia arrives at Troy. She is an exiled Thracian daughter of Ares and Amazon Otrera. Penthesileia makes an oath with Priam, who purifies her for her accidental killing of the Amazon queen Hippolyta.

Akhilleus kills her in the middle of her *aristeíā* (excellence on the battlefield). He lifts her helmet to see her face, feeling pity and love for her. The Greek soldier Thersites mocks him for his feelings, so Akhilleus slays him. This causes problems among the Greeks, as Thersites is Diomedes' kinsman. Akhilleus sails to Lesbos with Odysseus and is purified by Apollon, Artemis, and Leto.

The Eastern Son of Dawn, Memnon (an Aithiopian prince), arrives at Troy. He is the son of Eos, goddess of dawn, and the Trojan Tithonios. Like Akhilleus he wears armour made by

Hephaistos. The *kerostasia* (weighing of the *kēres* or "dooms") of Memnon and Akhilleus is done by Zeus to see which will win.

Through hepatoscopy (reading the liver of a sacrificial animal), Nestor divines that his son Antilokhos will die. He bids him farewell before they enter the fray. Nestor's horse is shot by Memnon, bringing the hero down. Antilokhos rescues him, but is killed by Memnon.

Akhilleus then kills Memnon. Memnon is flown away by Eos, who gains immortality for her son from Zeus. His body is buried in Aithiopia, while his immortal part lives either in Elysion or with his parents on the Eastern shore of Okeanos.

Akhilleus routs the Trojans, but is then killed by Paris and Apollon at the Skaian Gate of Troy. Apollon guides Paris' arrow, first landing a shot in Akhilleus' heel. This slows him down before a second, mortal wound is inflicted.

A fierce battle breaks out over the corpse of Akhilleus. The Greeks manage to take both the body and armour back to the ships. Aias kills Glaukos, then carries the body of Akhilleus while Odysseus fights a rear guard to protect him.

At Akhilleus' elaborate funeral, his mother Thetis, the Nereids, and the muses arrive and lament over his corpse. The winds (who are brothers of Memnon) are appeased in order to light Akhilleus' pyre. Thetis takes the immortal part of Akhilleus after the cremation to the Isle of Leuke (the White Island of Immortals in the North).

The Greeks pile the funeral mound and perform rites, including funeral games. Odysseus and Aias argue over the armour of Akhilleus. Odysseus wins with the help of Athena, and afterward Aias commits suicide.

The end of the *Aithiopis* is repeated at the beginning of the *Ilias Mikra*. It is an instance where scholars in Alexandria did not edit a seamless transition between poems.

ἡ Ἰλιὰς μικρά

Ilias Mikra

"I sing of Ilion and Dardania, the land of fine horses, wherein the Danai, followers of Ares, suffered many things."

Akhilleus' armour is awarded to Odysseus after Agamemnon asks the Trojan captives which of the heroes did them the most harm. Angered by this, Aias loses his mind and wishes to kill Agamemnon and Menelaos. Athena deflects his rage and Aias slaughters the cattle of the Akhaians, before committing suicide just before dawn.

Aias is said to be invulnerable in all places aside from his armpit, so Athena shows him this spot and he falls on his sword. Aias is buried in a coffin, not cremated. This is due both to the anger of Agamemnon and suicidal nature of his death.

A prophesy is revealed that Troy cannot fall without Philoktetes and his bow, given him by Herakles. Odysseus and Diomedes sail to Lemnos to retrieve him. Philoktetes is healed and then kills Paris in a duel. Menelaos mutilates his body in a characteristically epic act of vengeance.

The sons of Priam, Helenos and Deiphobos, quarrel over Helen, and when he loses, Helenos leaves Troy. Helen is married to Deiphobos (Paris' brother). Helenos is captured by Odysseus, and the seer tells the Greeks the conditions for the fall of Troy. Pelops' bones must be brought to them from Greece, Neoptolemos must fight, and the Palladion statue must be taken from Troy.

Eurypylos, son of Telephos of Mysia (grandson of Herakles and Priam), arrives. Fighting for the Trojans, he causes havoc on the battlefield. The Greeks have Pelops' bones sent to them. Odysseus and Diomedes fetch Neoptolemos from Skryos and give him Akhilleus' armour. Neoptolemos then kills Eurypylos.

Athena inspires Epeios to devise the Trojan Horse. Odysseus disguises himself and enters Troy; he is recognised by Helen, and they talk about the capture of the city. Then he kills some Trojans and escapes to the ships.

During the night, Odysseus and Diomedes steal the Palladion from Troy. The Greeks then place the best of their heroes inside the horse. The rest set fire to their huts and sail to Tenedos.

ἡ Ἰλίου πέρσις

Iliou Persis

"For their father the famous Earth Shaker gave both of them gifts, making each more glorious than the other."

The Trojans debate whether to burn the horse or dedicate it to Athena. They decide to demolish a section of the wall near the Skaian Gate and bring the horse into the city.

Laokoön's sons are killed by a pair of snakes from the sea; this omen leads Aineias to take his men away from Troy and stay on Mount Ida. He understands the snakes are sent by Athena because Laokoön insists that the Trojans burn the horse. Kassandra likewise predicts doom, but the Trojans pay her no heed.

Helen walks around the horse calling to the men inside in their wives' voices. Antilokos wants to answer, but Odysseus holds his mouth shut. Having entered Troy in disguise, Sinon sends a fire signal to the Greeks, who then set sail from Tenedos.

The heroes in the horse begin their night-time attack, capturing the city from within. Aineias rescues his father Ankhises, and the Greeks let the hero escape out of respect for his filial piety. Neoptolemos kills Priam at the altar of Zeus of the Hearth, where the king had fled for safety.

Menelaos kills Deiphobos, then draws his sword on Helen but drops it the moment he sees her breasts. He takes her back to the ships. Demophon and Akamas, sons of Theseus, find their grandmother Aithra and take her back with them.

The Greeks sack the whole city aside from the house of Antenor, who helped the embassy of Odysseus and Menelaos when they visited Troy. The infant son of Hektor, Astyanax, is thrown from the city walls. The Earth swallows Priam's most beautiful daughter Laodike.

Lokrian Aias rapes Kassandra, who holds onto the xoanon (cult statue) of Athena in the temple where she is the priestess. The statue falls and Kalkhas tells the Akhaians of Athena's wrath due to Lokrian Aias' act. The Greeks try Aias for this act, but he flees to the temple of Athena to avoid being stoned to death.

The Greeks give Kassandra to Agamemnon. They take no further action against Aias, incurring the wrath of Athena. Later, she wrecks much of the Greek fleet in retribution.

Akhilleus' shade appears and demands Priam's daughter Polyxena as his share of the spoils of war. She is dutifully sacrificed upon his tomb. Then Andromache is given to Neoptolemos, and Hekube to Odysseus.

οἱ Νόστοι

The *Nostoi*

"For gifts beguile men's minds and their deeds as well."

Athena causes Agamemnon and Menelaos to argue. Menelaos wants to set sail immediately. However, Agamemnon wants to appease Athena first.

Diomedes and Nestor sail home first, both arriving safely. Agamemnon remains at Troy in order to try and appease the goddess. Menelaos leaves next; he runs into a storm and loses all but five ships.

Kalkhas, Leonteus, Amphilokhos, Podaleiros, and Polypoites travel on foot to Kolophon. They are received by Mopsos, who defeats Kalkhas in a soothsaying contest. Kalkhas grows depressed and dies. He is buried by his comrades.

Akhilleus' ghost appears to Agamemnon to warn him of his future. Disregarding the ghost, Agamemnon makes the sacrifice and leaves. Agamemnon returns home, and is killed by

Aigisthos and Klytaimnestra. He is then avenged by Orestes and Pylades.

The rest set sail, and are almost entirely destroyed by a storm. At the Kapherian Rocks, Athena wrecks Aias the Lokrian's ships with Zeus' Thunderbolt and he drowns.

Following Thetis' advice, Neoptolemos makes the sacrifice and travels by land. He encounters Odysseus in Thrace, then travels to the land of the Mollosians where he becomes king. He hands over the kingship to Helenos, marrying him to his mother Deidameia. Neoptolemos takes over the kingship of Phthia after his grandfather Peleus' death.

Menelaos is driven off course, but sails through Libya, Phoenicia, Cyprus, and Egypt. He plunders during his journey, accumulating great wealth. After eight years, he returns home to Sparta with Helen.

ἡ Ὀδύσσεια

The *Odyssey*

"Sing to me of the man, Muse, the man of twists and turns driven time and again off course, once he had plundered the hallowed heights of Troy."

Odysseus arrives first at Ismaros and plunders the city. Then he reaches the Land of the Lotus Eaters, where his men forget themselves after tasting the lotus fruit (a narcotic). Odysseus drives them back to the ships, and they sail to the Land of the Kyklopes.

Entering a cave, the men find goats, which they sacrifice and eat. The kyklops Polyphemos arrives, trapping the men in the cave with a rock, as it is his home and they ate his goats. The kyklops proceeds to eat some of the men.

Odysseus gets Polyphemos drunk on wine and blinds him. Then he escapes the cave with his comrades. This incurs the wrath of the sea god Poseidon, who is Polyphemos' father.

At his next stop, Odysseus is given a cowhide bag containing the winds by Aiolos. He is given instructions on how to use them to return to Ithake. Just as he is about to land on his home shores, his men open the bag, as they believe it contains treasure. The winds are all released, sending the ships back to Aiolos. This time the Keeper of the Winds cannot help them, as he has been forbidden to do so by the gods.

They sail on to the land of the cannibalistic Laistrygonians, who eat the men. Only Odysseus and the crew of his ship escape. They arrive on Kirke the sorceress' island of Aiaia, and she changes the men into animals. Odysseus is immune due to the moly plant given him by Hermes. He threatens Kirke, who changes his men back and makes an oath not to harm them. Afterward, Odysseus sleeps with Kirke.

Following a year with her, he sails to Okeanos and visits the Underworld as per her instruction. The shade of the Theban seer Teiresias prophesies his future. He tells Odysseus not to eat the Cattle of Helios on his journey home, and that he will arrive home alone and on another king's ship to find his home overrun with suitors.

Teiresias also tells him that, after dealing with his problems in Ithake, he must travel to a land where men eat their food with no salt and know nothing of the sea. There, he must make sacrifices to Poseidon before he can return home and live in peace until his death as an old man.

Odysseus then returns to Kirke before sailing out again. He passes the Sirens, who lure sailors to their death with songs of the past. Stopping up the ears of his crew with wax, he is tied to the mast so he can hear their song. They sing of Troy to Odysseus, which makes his heart ache with nostalgia.

Next, the ship threads the route between the monster Skylla and the whirlpool Kharybdis. Before they pass through, Skylla eats six of his men.

They next come to Thrinakia. Despite his warnings, Odysseus' crew feast on the herds of the sun god Helios. Zeus then wrecks the ship with a Thunderbolt. Holding onto the mast, Odysseus is sent back to Kharybdis. He grabs the branch of a fig tree above the whirlpool just before it swallows the mast.

When Kharybdis spits the mast out, he jumps onto it and is carried to the island of Ogygia. There he is welcomed by the nymph Kalypso. He stays with her for seven years.

At this time, the suitors have assembled at Odysseus' palace, seeking the hand of his wife Penelope. Believing the hero dead, they feast continuously while Telemakhos anguishes over his father's fate. The young hero leaves to find news of his father, travelling to Pylos to talk with Nestor, then Sparta to talk with Menelaos. After, he returns to Ithake.

Odysseus builds a raft and puts out to sea. Poseidon breaks up the raft, and Odysseus is washed up naked on the shores of Phaiakia. He is welcomed by the king of the Phaiakians, Alkinoös. After being given gifts, he is sent home on a Phaiakian ship.

Arriving at Ithake, Athena tells him of the situation with the suitors and his wife. He enters his home disguised as a beggar, revealing his identity only to his son, his slave Eumaios, and his cowherd Philoitios. Penelope devises a plot where she will agree to marry the suitor who can string the mighty bow of Odysseus and shoot it.

After they all fail, Odysseus obtains the bow, strings it, and begins to shoot the suitors. Odysseus slaughters all the suitors with the help of Athena, Telemakhos, Eumaios, and Philoitios. He executes the traitors in his house before revealing his identity to his wife and then his father.

ἡ Τηλεγόνεια

The *Telegony*

"He ravenously devoured boundless meat and delicious wine."

The suitors are buried, and Odysseus sacrifices to the nymphs. He then sails to Elis to visit his herds. He is entertained by Augias' grandson Polyxenos, a comrade of his during the Trojan War.

Odysseus next travels by foot though Epiros. There the Oracle of Zeus at Dodona predicts that he will be killed by the hand of his own son.

Reaching the land of the Thesprotians he performs the sacrifices enjoined by Teiresias, appeasing Poseidon and completing his sacrificial orders. Odysseus marries Kallidike, queen of the Thesprotians. He leads the Thesprotians against their neighbours, the Brygoi. Ares routs the Thesprotians, but Athena comes to Odysseus' aid.

Apollon breaks up the fight. Kallidike dies and her son by Odysseus, Polypoites, becomes king. Odysseus sails back to Ithake where he meets his second son by Penelope, Polyporthes.

His son by Kirke, Telegonos, grows up during this time. Searching for his father, Telegonos arrives at Ithake and starts to ravage the island. Odysseus goes out to fight him and is slain by Telegonos, who does not recognise him. The spear he uses is barbed with a stingray spine, which provides the gentle death from the sea as an old man, predicted for Odysseus by Teiresias.

Telegonos, Telemakhos, and Penelope take Odysseus' corpse to Kirke's island for burial. After the funeral rites for Odysseus Kirke makes the three of them immortal. Telemakhos marries Kirke, and Telegonos marries Penelope.

Part III: The Heroic Ideal

ὁ κόσμος Ὁμηρικός

Homer's World

The world of Homer is divorced from any specific historical era. It is made up of deep layers of Indo-European warrior culture. It espouses Northern ideals – those of a mobile heroic culture surviving in a settled environment.

While Hesiod spoke from a demotic 8th century BCE perspective, Homer's is a timeless aristocratic world set against the backdrop of the Mykenaian Bronze Age. Homer paints a picture of a powerful feudal society where heroic lords hold power through might, enforcing their right to rule in the noble ranks as "first among equals."

Homer's heroes stride boldly through their world, fearing neither gods nor men. The future does not oppress them, even if it holds impending doom. Homer focusses on the nobles, the *āristoi* ("the best"). The common man, while present, is irrelevant. Each hero brings with him a common army, but it is his actions, not theirs, that are decisive. His *monomakhía* ("single combat") is what matters.

Everything pivots on honour, virtue, strength, bravery, courage, and prowess. The only weakness is cowardice: the failure to pursue heroic goals. Hero has no feminine gender – all heroes are men. There is a sharp divide between *āristoi* and *dêmos* ("the people"), the elect few and the many. There is no social conscience, no responsibility other than familial; no obligation to anyone or anything other than one's own prowess and drive to victory and power.

Greek kings had ceased to exist by the time Homer's poems were committed to writing. The nobles ruled without a "first among equals," and the *dêmos'* menacing influence was starting to rear its head. The common mob were learning of their potential power.

Honour

In Homer, the words "warrior" and "hero" are synonymous. Thus, the concept of honour is the highest value in Homeric society. The entire culture is built on honour and prowess; every action, every judgement defines or realises honour.

Honour is individual to the hero; he fights only for honour and himself. Honour is likewise reserved for the elite. If all may obtain equal honour, there is no honour for anyone.

In the *Iliad*, both Akhilleus and Hektor know they are doomed. However, the call of honour demands they obey the heroic code without hesitation or question. It is more valuable to them than their mortal existence.

This unwritten code of honour permeates all actions of the heroes in the *Iliad*. Heroism brings honour and fame, not happiness. Death on the battlefield is more honourable than inglorious old age.

When Agamemnon takes Briseis from Akhilleus, he shames the hero's honour. Akhilleus withdraws from the fight, as the slight on his honour is so great it is worth all the honour he could accrue in the entire war. When Akhilleus refuses the penal gift of Agamemnon he breaches the heroic code, but vindicates his honour with a full display of prowess upon his return to the battlefield.

His fury leads him to keep the body of Hektor long after the reasonable period of time, putting a dark mark on his honour in the eyes of the gods. When he returns Hektor's body to Priam, he expunges his wrath and regains his honour. He wipes the slate clean.

Monomakhía ("individual combat") offers the highest honour. Who the hero fights, how he fights, and how he fares are all important factors in determining his honour. Victory without honour is unacceptable.

Honour requires public proclamation, and this requires evidence. A trophy from the fight is an indisputable measure of success. In Homer, a fallen enemy's armour replaces the head taken in more ancient times.

The armour of Akhilleus changes hands from Patroklos to Hektor, then back to Akhilleus as each victor takes his trophy, declaring his prowess. During the funeral games of Patroklos, Diomedes takes his prizes after the chariot race. He is filled with pride for his manliness. Concrete expressions of honour are treasures of intrinsic value, since they provide evidence of *aristeíā* ("excellence" on the battlefield).

In this honour culture, when a dispute arises, swearing an oath to their claim is final. If it is false, the gods will punish the offender; no man has the right to raise a charge of false swearing. If the hero does not wish to swear an oath, then trial by arbitration or combat are the only other ways to settle disputes over rights among the heroic class.

Feasting

Feasting is what occupies the hero when he is not on the battlefield. This is not a gluttonous act, but a ritual performance. It empowers bonds with the gods and other men.

Feasting is a sacrificial act. All animals eaten are first sacrificed. The word *daïs* means both feast and sacrifice, as well as implying the distribution of meat.

The feast is shared with the gods, as it is sacrificial, meaning it cannot be refused. If invited to feast, the hero is obligated to attend. If a *xénos* ("stranger" or "guest") arrives at the hero's home or camp he is seated, honoured, and feasted; only after a meal is it proper for a host to enquire about who his guest is and the nature of his mission. Through sharing food, a bond is created or renewed tying men and gods, living and dead, into an ordered Cosmos of existence.

There is a distinct order to the events. The sacrificial fire must be burning. Barley is first thrown into the fire, then the animal (cow, goat, sheep, or pig) is killed with an axe and a knife.

The thigh bones are stripped out, along with some fat and the gall bladder. These are given to the gods as their share on the sacrificial fire. The thigh bones are wrapped in two layers of fat, then cast onto the fire along with the gall bladder. The organs are then cooked on the sacrificial fire and eaten.

Finally, the carcass is taken away and the meat cut up. It is then skewered and roasted on the domestic fire (the firstlings of meat are often also cast into the flames for the gods). Before the meat is distributed, small dishes of vegetables and bread are served.

The allotment of meat is important, as different parts of the animal carry higher or lower status, and are handed out to the feasting heroes accordingly. The rightful shares are allotted as are spoils of war. Those who lead in battle get the choicest cuts; the *daïs* lies at the heart of the heroic power structure.

Power

Blood distinction and birth are of the highest importance to Homeric heroes. Nobility is passed down hereditary lines, and the heroes' genealogy is recounted in the epics. A clear caste system is in place, with the ruling warrior class at the top.

Among these warriors is a *wánax* (king, lord, or chief) who leads them. The king is father to the community. Like Zeus, he is patriarch.

A king is an agent of the community principle. He is arbiter of disputes, commander-in-chief, host of dinners and councils. The king is also a military leader and offers protection, which is the extent of his role to the common people.

The king in heroic society does not have arbitrary authority. To the nobles he is "first among equals." This is because there is no royal blood, just noble blood.

The king rules "by might." Might does not imply tyranny, but strength and power: authority to rule. Authority is secured by exercising authority, and status by displaying status.

The king gains by exercising what he already has. To continue this upward trajectory, he has to make the correct sacrifices; he must give the gods their share. By doing this, he expresses gratitude for his success, as hubris will reverse his momentum.

Since kingship is not automatically passed from father to son, the throne is open to struggle among the nobility. One needs the might to rule. A weak king will not last, as power struggle is present at all times.

An old king relies on strong sons to keep him in his position until he dies, or is able to pass his rule to them due to their might. When selecting an heir, his own sons might not be up to the role. In these instances, the king may go outside his kingdom to find a suitable successor.

In the *Iliad*, Odysseus and Nestor struggle to maintain Agamemnon's authority. This is not through personal loyalty, but as he is a channel through which policy can be made coherent and effective. Agamemnon is not a good king according to the criteria. These are above all to be responsive and authoritative; to hear good counsel, and convert it into policy by sealing it with his personal approval.

On the contrary, Agamemnon is weak, depressed, anxious, and unfair. He is a good warrior, but poor king; the role is beyond his personal power. Agamemnon fails to understand he is not allowed to follow his personal inclinations. A king has more power than other heroes, but less freedom.

Heroes in battle act as individuals, choosing when to fight and who their opponents are. No one commands or gives orders. In the *Iliad*, Agamemnon is in charge as his status is highest, having brought the largest force (and he is also brother to the aggrieved party). However, he does not command other heroes in regard to their battlefield conduct, but acts as a rallying flag for the cause as a whole.

Preeminence lies in the *oîkos*: the large noble household with its staff of slaves and commoners, as well as aristocratic retainers, along with allies among relatives and *xénoi* (guest-friends). Each of the *oîkoi* (households) vie with each other for greater wealth, power, superior status, and kingship. The magnitude of the *oîkos* and number of retainers supported directly correlate to the amount of power a lord wields. There is no specific palace, and if the crown changes hands, the new king rules from his own *oîkos*.

In the *Odyssey*, if Penelope had gone with a suitor to his home, he would have been king; but Telemachos would have kept Odysseus' *oîkos*. The *oîkos* is the household and lands that personally belong to a noble family. It is what entitles them to be of the aristocratic class.

Aside from his own *oîkos*, the king has a separate *témenos* (estate) at his disposal, which comes with the crown. The *témenos* accompanies the title of king. *Témenos* is also used to describe the temple estate: a sacred precinct or grove set aside for the enjoyment of the god.

Odysseus does not automatically resume his position as king, but must fight to regain it, proving his might to rule. Penelope does not rule in Odysseus' absence, as the queen can only have an advisory role to the king. Telemakhos (a youth) does not have the might to rule. The wife of a former king does not decide who rules; but if Penelope shares her bed with a suitor, a shadow of legitimacy passes to him and he can then lay claim to the throne.

The decision of who rules lies with the gods, but the hero directs this decision with the power of his might. Odysseus strings the bow and slaughters the suitors, displaying his might to rule. He counts on his kin and household to aid him – royal power is personal power.

Alliances are made between families, not communities. Marriage is key to these power alliances, and genealogies are memorised in order to preserve them. The source of noble power is personal relationships, not state relationships. Power lies in

Menelaos, for instance, not Sparta. It rests with Agamemnon, not Mykenai; Odysseus, not Ithake.

Kin ties are the net of power wielded by Akhaian lords. The poets display intimate knowledge of heroes' traditional family lineages. The myth establishes bloodlines, which are critically important to *āristoi*. Loyalty to family supersedes loyalty to social class.

A family is responsible for punishing the offender in criminal cases, not the public. This is because even homicide is not a public offence. The ability to pursue blood vengeance is linked to the strength of the household and family.

Therápōn (retainer) is a loose word defining nobles who are attached to a chieftain or king. A *therápōn* is a second in command, like Meriones is to Idomeneos in the *Iliad*. Patroklos is Akhilleus' *therápōn*.

The *therápōn* holds a personal relationship of obligation. A lord may have a number of retainers in his household. *Therápōn* also carries a meaning of "ritual substitute," tying them deeply to the personality of the lord.

While class, kin, and *oîkos* are three overlapping loyalty groups, guest-friendship is also a very serious institution. *Xénos* means "foreigner," "stranger," "host," and "guest-friend." It is a formal relationship.

The stranger is looked at with distrust; he is not safe and has no rights. However, they must be given hospitality in the home they visit. Once they are received into the home, they cannot be harmed, must be honoured, and become a guest-friend. There is in the guest-host relationship a rapid oscillation between fear, lavish entertainment, and complete trust.

The stranger himself is also bound to the same rules and may not harm his host. He must also honour the newly established relationship. This relationship is hereditary, and the ancestors of *xénoi* have the same obligations to each other.

A hero who has a *xénos* in a foreign land has an effective substitute for a kinsman. He has refuge. *Xénoi* can also be called upon in times of war, but with no guarantee.

The *boulé* (assembly) is an inheritance from older, Indo-European tribal nomadic culture. For this gathering, heads of the noble *oîkoi* are summoned by the king to discuss public matters. During times of war, a *boulé* can be called in camp to discuss matters as well.

When Telemakhos assembles a *boulé* in the *Odyssey*, it has been twenty years since the last was called. Akhilleus also calls a *boulé* in the *Iliad*. Neither of these are conventional, as only the king has the right to call the assembly.

The time of the *boulé* is always dawn, and only the matter at hand is discussed. Whoever is moved to talk holds the herald's sceptre while speaking. The sceptre, like that of the god Hermes, is a magic wand rendering the speaker inviolate.

No vote is cast during this meeting. The *boulé* merely gives king or commander a lay of the sentiment. He then makes the decision on his own.

Wealth

The ethics of the Age of Heroes prevent the practice of trade as a vocation. There is not a single word in the *Iliad* or *Odyssey* for "merchant." The Phoenicians are traders and provisioners, not Greeks.

Profit is an alien concept, and it is taboo to gain in an exchange. Peasants can barter, but not make profit. They can exchange labour for goods.

Control over one's labour constitutes freedom. If he wills, Odysseus can plough and perform other tasks. However, he does not have to, as he is master of the house.

There is a difference between aristocracy joining in labour when they choose to, and those who are compelled to. In this way, choice is key in separating freeman from servant.

Gain belongs to the world of raiding and warfare where it is acquired through prowess, not manipulation or bargaining. War and raiding are one and the same – no distinction is made between them. Wars are fought for booty, not territory.

Raids are organised by an *oîkos* or a group of *oîkoi*. The captain of the raid distributes booty to participants in correct portions. The king gains the larger share, while others draw lots.

Agamemnon flouts this custom at the beginning of the *Iliad*. It starts the trouble with Akhilleus, as his rightful distribution is taken from him. Agamemnon can do this despite being inferior in prowess to Akhilleus, as he is superior by right of position.

The wealth sought by raiders is women, cattle, and treasure. When a city has been sacked, women and children are taken as slaves and men killed or ransomed. Persons and property of the slain are taken by the victor; these are known as *géras* (prize or privilege), a word used for a trophy, war bride, mark of honour, or funeral. The offspring of slaves are not slaves, but members of the *oîkos*, as they are sired by the lord or a member of his family. There is no stigma attached to illegitimate children.

The heroic culture of Homer is a pastoral culture – a cattle culture. There is little agricultural activity. The minimal tillage is mostly used for vines and orchards.

Homer's world displays all the signs of an Indo-European Steppe warrior world. Cattle are the preferred currency between man and the divine; they are the measuring stick of worth in a realm with no coins. Cattle are not the medium of exchange, but simply its measure (an item is "worth twenty oxen" for example).

Bride price, gift exchange, and raiding are all part of cattle culture. The herd and wealth increases, yet each member of the herd will die, making wealth expendable. It must be used, not accumulated for its own sake. Cattle wealth becomes social capital through feasting and distribution of meat. Heroes steal cattle by raiding, then sacrifice them to the gods, swear mighty oaths over the carcasses, and feast with guests and allies.

Bronze, iron, and gold treasures are given as gifts. They are stored unused in the *oîkos* storerooms until such a time as they are given away. They are symbols of prestige to be re-gifted in turn. Gift-giving is always the first half of a reciprocal action: counter-giving. This gift-exchange is at the centre of heroic diplomacy.

In the *Odyssey*, the suitors ultimately want Odysseus' cattle wealth. This is because Penelope and the king's cattle are one and the same.

When Telemakhos visits the palaces of Nestor and Menelaos, he is welcomed very differently in each. Nestor is more pious than Menelaos, and his hospitality more fitting and correct for a hero. Nestor's wealth is cattle and modest goods, while Menelaos has boundless material wealth.

Cattle wealth is acceptable wealth that can be put to good use. Material wealth requires much effort and leads to no socially beneficial end. Cattle wealth is honourable; material wealth is suspect. True wealth is measured in cattle – in social worth.

Horses also form an important part of heroic wealth and are again a reflection of Indo-European Steppe culture. Horses feature heavily in the *Iliad*, but are not ridden. Chariots are used as transportation to the battlefield, but not in the traditional manner. In the Greek heroic age, the ship is the sea chariot on the liquid Steppe and second vehicle of heroes.

The epithet "breaker of horses" is used of many heroes including Diomedes and Hektor. An Anatolian Indo-European people, the Trojans are renowned horsemen. The finest horses in epic belong to the Thracians, however.

The horse is the spirit of the North: whiter than snow, as fast as the wind, shining like the sun. The horse and hero are one and the same. The wooden horse is the one gift the Greeks know Trojans cannot resist. It is a holy effigy: a god.

Gods

Blood of gods flows through heroes' veins. The beauty of the gods is reflected in the hero, who is *kalós* (beautiful) – this is both physical beauty and personal quality. Beauty is intrinsically linked to heroism and power, with thick, lustrous hair an emblem of the hero. Like the gods, the hero's hands are where his destructive power is concentrated.

Gods and heroes mirror each other with the same concerns over honour and prowess. Heroes cannot replace the gods, as they do not have the power to do so. Gods cannot die, so they cannot be heroes.

Certain gods have an enhanced standing in the Age of Heroes. Most prominent is the thundering Sky Father, Zeus. He is not omnipotent or omnipresent, but his power is without equal.

Zeus alone does not directly act in the material world, but instead works through the other gods. Ares and Athena have prominent roles as war gods; Apollon and Artemis are destroyers too, but from afar. Hermes is psychopomp (guide of souls). Hera, queen of the gods, is a pivotal power in the *Iliad*, since her anger against Troy is absolute. Poseidon as "Earth Shaker" and sea god is a potent force also, and he likewise plays a prominent role in the *Odyssey*.

Gods such as the grain mother Demeter and god of ecstasy Dionysos are unimportant to the Age of Heroes. They resurface in the Age of Iron after a hiatus. In the violent world of *āristoi*, the aristocratic Apollon is honoured more than Dionysos, a god of the *dêmos* (common people).

Olympian gods did not create the world. Thus, they are not responsible for it. They are likewise neither good nor evil, since they have no ethical quality.

The hero never turns to the gods for ethical guidance. He can neither sin, nor atone; he has no feeling of moral guilt towards the gods, as morality is manmade. There is no grand Cosmic justice – favour, not merit, determines the gifts of gods to men.

Gods are not feared any more than a mortal overlord, so there is no reverential fear of them by the hero. Gods are not agents of justice, but will punish *húbris* (arrogance against the gods). Like men, they are quick to resent a slight and do not like men boasting their skills are better. They punish perjury – not because they care about man's lies, but they will not allow their names to be taken in vain.

The *Iliad* has no word for "god-fearing." Neither work has a word meaning the "love of god" either.

Death

Homer's funeral rites are those of Steppe culture. Cremation on a huge pyre, and the heaping of an imposing *túmbos* (burial mound) harkens back to extremely ancient practices. The *kêdeia* (funeral) is a display of wealth, status, kin-solidarity, and family pride. The *túmbos* memorialises the burial of the great dead; it is the earth equivalent of epic poem.

The body of the hero is washed, oiled, purified with flour if wounded, and shrouded. A huge pile of wood is gathered, then the bier of the hero placed on top. Suet is used to help the fire burn.

Once the body is cremated, the embers are quenched and bones washed in wine. They are then wrapped in fat and placed in a vessel. This vessel is buried deep and piled high with stones and earth so no change can come to them. The bones of great men possess the power of the dead heroes and are sought out. Hero cults worship at the mounds containing these powerful remains.

Each man has a *kēr* ("doom" or "fate of death") that watches him hungrily. It has an interest in his death, leading him to it and wishing to devour his blood. *Kēres* have teeth, wings, and talons. They are composites of dogs and birds; the battlefield scavengers that eat the dead and dying heroes.

If the dead warrior is not recovered by his people, he will be treated like a dead animal: disposed of and eaten by scavengers. Frenzied battles rage over the corpse of a slain hero. His enemies wish to throw his corpse to the dogs, and his allies want to give him a grand funeral. The funeral prevents organic death; the *kēres* present an opposing image.

Rotting is unclean, while burning is clean. Through cremation, the body is spared decay. Like the *holokaumata* (sacrifice to the dead), cremation consumes the entire body of a hero, allowing his Spirit to escape its mortal confines. The body, which was sustained by *ménos* (internal fire), is returned to pure *ménos* (the sacrificial fire).

Psykhê (soul) is the image of the man. Once it leaves, the body rots and changes form, going back to nature. The funeral releases the *psykhê*, which has no function other than to leave the body at death.

The dead hero is thought of as departing on a journey. His *skiá* ("shadow"), or *eidôlon* (image), goes to the Underworld to join the tribes of the dead. The *eidôlon* lives in the Underworld as a frozen, unchanging image of the human at the moment of death.

Shades of regular dead must be summoned by the living in order to speak, but heroic dead can make themselves appear on occasion. They are able to do this both in the dream and waking worlds. The great heroes have both a shade in the Underworld, ruled by Hades, and an undying Spirit in heroic paradise.

At the end of the Thebais, Kapaneus' wife throws herself on his funeral pyre so as to accompany him to the heroic otherworld. This, along with the sacrifice of animals or humans on the pyre, is an Indo-European custom found also in Thrace, India, and Scandinavia. In the *Iliad*, Trojan captives are killed over the pyre of Patroklos so they can join him in death. Similarly, Polyxena is killed at the tumulus of Akhilleus so she can be his posthumous war bride.

The hero does not take his possessions with him. His most treasured possessions are prizes at his funeral games. His compatriots vie to win them through feats of strength and warrior skills.

The prize is a memory of the hero. It is won by another hero through a memorable act. The competitor attains fame through his victory, making the funeral famous as he recounts his victory to others.

ἡρωικό διάνοια

Heroic Mindset

To understand the hero, it is vital to understand the heroic mindset. The hero is defined by several interlinked psychological and extra-somatic qualities, which are known and understood instinctively by those in the heroic warband. The Homeric works in Greek use several potent concepts that are often lost in translation.

The stories of heroes are called *kléa andrōn* ("fames of men"). *Kléos* (fame, glory, news) is sought after by the hero. Not only men, but objects can be *klutá* (famous). Armour is famous if won on the battlefield, bestowing *kléos* on the winner; men remember famous gifts exchanged between heroes. *Kléos* is won through action, and proven with *géras* (prize or booty).

Kûdos (glory of victory) is lustre belonging to the successful. *Kûdos* is won only by a living individual, whereas *kléos* is shared by the hero's father and with ancestral dead. *Kûdos* is only for men and is only positive. *Kléos* can be negative, since it is one's reputation; it is what others say of the hero.

Tīmḗ (honour) is one's valuation by others. It means not only honour, but also status, price, and penalty. It is a hero's worth in the eyes of his peers. *Tīmḗ* is quantitative, whereas *kléos* is qualitative: the description of a man.

A hero with a high *kûdos* also has high *tīmḗ*. *Kûdos* is absolute, like health or strength. *Tīmḗ*, on the other hand, is relative. It is a measure of standing compared to others. *Tīmḗ* awarded to one man must be withdrawn from others.

Both *kûdos* and *tīmḗ* fluctuate continuously. Men gain *tīmḗ*; they give the gods *tīmḗ*. The gods took *tīmaí* (honours) from the Titans by way of *bíē* (might). When mortals fail to give *tīmaí* to the gods, their status lowers – like men of the Silver Age.

Kléos is the hero's social identity. It is his epitaph. Through his actions, a hero creates his own memorial.

Bíē is prerequisite to *kléos*; it is a necessary component of the hero. Without *bíē*, man is not a hero. *Bíē* is dangerous if unchecked and not balanced with *dikē* (justice). It can lead a hero to make rash, violent, irreversible decisions.

Aristeíā is prestige: the summit of happiness for a hero. It is his excellence on the battlefield. In his *aristeíā* – his power drive towards supremacy, his best moment, his excellence – the hero proves he is worthy of the title *āristos* ("best" or champion).

Aretē is virtue or excellence. *Aretē* is full realisation of a hero's potential. It is the heroic ideal – its *télos* (ultimate goal).

Ménos means impulse. It is a feeling of strength and braveness – a single vitality, both somatic and psychic, expressed in vigour. It is the inner fire of the hero.

Ménos is not a permanent fixture like *thumós* (Spirit) or *nóos* (vision). It is breathed into heroes by the gods. A hero feels the energy of *ménos* enter his *thumós*. The *ménos* Athena breathes into Diomedes allows him to see the gods and fight them with impunity. *Ménos* is often gained after an invocation and, like *atē* (desire), it is a hypernormal state.

Ménos is the quality of winds and rivers. The *ménos* of the sun is heat. *Ménos* is fire – pure energy. *Ménos* is rage, and the fire of *ménos* can, while functioning, be seen in the eyes of a hero.

Ménos must be fed food and drink, as it is the metabolic fire also. *Ménos* is in the organs and the conscious, and vital to a well-functioning body. The living man is one piece, and all processes are aspects of a single functioning: *ménos*.

Fire is pure motion; it is matter in the process of transformation. It both burns and tempers iron. *Ménos* makes the hero hard tempered, giving him the power to move and to resist. Book twenty of the *Iliad* says of Akhilleus that his hands are like fire, his *ménos* is like iron. Hardness and heat are combined; strength is energy, strength is iron.

Ménos makes the hero stand firm when all is in flux. It is the ability for stillness, keeping a hero unshaken and steady. Due to his *ménos* he does not flinch or tremble.

In *Iliad* book fifteen, Hector goes berserk with *ménos*. It becomes *lússā* (wolfishness), the doglike rabid state. It is one in which the warrior respects neither gods nor men. Hektor goes too far and is "mad like Ares."

Lússā is the heat of *ménos* raised too high. The warrior foams at the mouth and shakes all over. Hektor becomes increasingly violent through the *Iliad* – unbalanced and overly confident. He degenerates into a bestial state. *Lússā* descends only on Hektor and Akhilleus. To Hektor it is a weakness, but to Akhilleus it is a strength.

Akhilleus experiences first *mênis* (anger) at the actions of Agamemnon, then *khólos* (rage) towards Hektor after the death of Patroklos. *Khólos* is a whole-body reaction that drives men to violent speech and action. *Khólos* can be "poured" into a violent action, or it can be "digested" and in time the man will regain his calm.

Lússā, *mênis*, and *khólos* are all manifestations of *ménos*. *Ménos* shares the same root as the Indic mánas ("mind"); it is linked with memory. When reminded of his father, Telemakhos is filled with *ménos*. Sleep separates men from *ménos* briefly, and the dead have no *ménos*. The *haimakouría* ("blood sacrifice") – like that given the dead by Odysseus in the *Odyssey* – briefly bestows a pseudo-*ménos*.

Thumós can be used the way modern people use "heart." It means breath soul or life soul. It fulfils the function of an organ of feeling.

Thumós tells a man when to eat or when to kill. It advises him on the course of action and puts words into his mouth. He converses with it as an independent inner voice. *Thumós* abides in the *stéthos* (chest), seat of thought.

Thumós is the hero's Spirit. It is the seat of passions, wishes, hopes, and inclinations. It is not an organ, but a substance that fills the *phrénes* (lungs or wits).

Thumós is breath as distinguished from air, which is converted to breath by the organism. *Thumós* is organic air: hot, wet, and in motion. The fire of *ménos* combines with *thumós* to fill the body with steam.

When a god inspires a hero, he breathes *ménos* into him. This is like blowing on a fire, breathing confidence into his *thumós*. It increases the heat and density of the hero's steam.

The hero maintains himself because of his *ménos*, but can act responsively because of his *thumós*. *Thumós* is the seat of all practical conscious – it is practical intelligence. *Thumós*, like *ménos*, only exists within a living hero's body. *Ménos* is broken up at death; *Thumós* becomes air on exhalation.

Nóos is vision, but not sight. *Nóos* catches an unspoken signal; it is recognition and responsive understanding. Sight takes in the thing, but *nóos* sees its meaning. *Nóos* is recognition of meaning in things perceived of or imagined – a theoretical faculty.

Nóos is also connected to words and a source of mythos. *Nóos* is related to plans and intentions. Unspoken words are concealed in *nóos*. *Nóos* grasps meaning immediately; it is the understanding of an individual knower.

All men have a different *nóos*, as it is their individual perception and understanding. *Nóos* allows the hero to utilise *mêtis* (strategy). *Mêtis* is how a hero can make considered actions, rather than thoughtlessly exercising his *bíē* (might).

If *thumós* is consciousness of a being, *nóos* is that of the Cosmos. *Thumós* is inner, *nóos* is outer. Yet *nóos* also resides in man, located (like *thumós*) in the *stēthos* and *phrénes*.

Nóos is passive and *ménos* cannot enter it. *Thumós* involves intention and inclination: it is active. *Nóos* is detached, while *thumós* is individual. *Thumós* exists in men and animals, but *nóos* only in men. *Ménos, thumós,* and *nóos* are functions of each other, and all are mortal.

Psykhê is the eschatological soul. Its only function is to leave the man upon death. *Psykhê, thumós, nóos,* and *ménos* are all types of mortal soul.

Upon death, what remain of a man are *psykhê* as an *eidôlon* (image) and *sōma* (body). Mortal man is divided into matter and form: *sōma* and *psykhê*. While the *stēthos* (chest) is the seat of consciousness, the head is the seat of *psykhê*. The *eidôlon* is a head without *ménos*. *Psykhê* can only speak in dreams or when fed hot blood, attaining pseudo-*ménos*.

Autos ("himself") is not *psykhê*, which is in the underworld. *Autos* is the feast for dogs after death; these are cremated physical remains. *Autos* and *psykhê* are separated upon death. The concepts of *thumós, ménos,* and *psykhê* in relation to their function after death have cognates in the Indic tradition.

A witless action is always, without doubt, a god's intervention. Irrational actions are works of the gods. When Agamemnon takes Briseis, it is because of *atē* (desire). This is the gods' doing, and it in turn fires Akhilleus' *thumós*.

The gods take away a man's "understanding," rendering him "senseless." This is *atē*: a temporary clouding of the mind. It is a short-lived, partial insanity causing the hero to act poorly, or allow foolish words to escape the barrier of his teeth. It is caused by an external "daimonic" agent, but is not a form of punishment.

Atē means "error" or "delusion." It is personified by the blinding goddess of ruin, daughter of Zeus. The word implies wrongness and wickedness.

Atē is imposed upon the hero by limitations or contradictions of his culture. His cultural resources are inadequate to the demands of his action. He often does the wrong thing at the very moment he is trying harder to do right.

Yet it is just that those who do wrong suffer, and the *atē* of a good man is still *atē*. An excellent man accepts life's consequences with no sense of guilt or sin. Instead, there is shame or pollution by another's actions. Purity is not attached to morality in the heroic world.

The Homeric *daímōn* is not the personal *daímōn* of later Greek thought. This role is played by *moíra* (portion or fate). The later development of *daímōn* came with an increasing feeling of helplessness. This has no place in the thoughts of aristocratic heroes.

Daímōn is simply an unspecified superhuman force – an uncanny, homogeneous reservoir of power. It is an undefined external influence that cannot squarely be placed on *dîos* or *theós* (a specific god). *Daímōn* is an external factor, which does not manifest in the *phrénes* or *stēthos*. Bad acts and thoughts are attributed to a *daimōn*.

Atē and *daímōn* are not normal to the mind, and enter the hero suddenly. *Atē, ménos*, and *daímōn* are not part of the Self, as they are not consciously in a hero's control. In the *Odyssey*, all monitions are the work of the gods. Acts of memory, seeing clearly, foolish ideas – the gods are in all these. Every human action and idea could be the direct consequence of divine intervention.

If *tīmē* (honour) is public esteem and the highest good, aversion to *aidōs* (shame) is the strongest moral force. *Aidōs* is both disgrace and fear of disgrace; it is a hero's sense of propriety. *Némesis* is a feeling of outrage: righteous indignation.

Paris accepts himself as he is. He knows his weaknesses, but does not try to improve himself. He is insensitive to *némesis* and has no shame.

Aidōs anticipates *némesis*, thus preventing unwise action. *Némesis* drives one to attack those who have not shown appropriate *aidōs*. It is provoked by any improper and unexpected act, such as failure of tact, cowardice, or betrayal.

Aidōs and *némesis* are inner and outer aspects of the same thing, and connected mostly with the three main social situations that test morality. In a sexual situation, self-indulgence is a shameful act; when entertaining guests, miserliness is unacceptable; on the battlefield, cowardice is disgraceful. Of these, combat is the most important social situation, since more is at stake.

The English renderings of Homer cannot adequately deliver the complexity of this heroic mindset. The forces mixing and opposing each other make a complex web of extra-somatic qualities. They all influence a hero and his actions.

Each hero is a particular mix of these forces. The way he utilises his own strengths and weaknesses defines how he operates within the cosmos. To deny that which is latent within him would be folly, but to allow negative forces to take control would be equally as disastrous.

The hero aims to bring these forces into balance. By understanding them, he gains understanding of himself. He can then mould his raw clay into a vessel of transcendence.

ἡρωικόν ἀρχέτυπον

Heroic Archetypes

Homer presents us with several heroic archetypes. There is the powerful, but fragile-minded Aias; feisty and wily Diomedes; over-confident and tragic Hektor; wise Nestor; and gentle Menelaos – to name but a few. Of the heroes, two are of special interest, being thematic of the two Homeric works.

Though absent for much of it, Akhilleus is the *Iliad's* key hero. It is his story. This youthful hero is unsurpassed in might and inner fire. He is the pure warrior with an immortal streak, traversing the Solar Path and seeking his place among the gods.

Odysseus is the *Odyssey's* main character. He is the mature hero who relies on his wits. His understanding is crucial to success on his journey.

Odysseus goes beyond the role of warrior. He must operate in the otherworldly extremities of the Cosmos in order to make his return home to the Polar North.

These two heroic archetypes lay out a schema, a plan, a map that we can follow today. They complement each other, both showing a way for the hero through two different stages of his life. The youthful and mature hero archetypes allow us to emulate the ancients, drawing upon their wisdom not only to defeat enemies blocking our way, but also go beyond and return to our true Home.

This is not the way for everyone. It is for the *āristoi*. Only the elite can hope to succeed.

Ἀχιλλεύς

Akhilleus

Akhilleus epitomizes the heroic warrior youth. He embodies everything associated with a glorious hero on the battlefield.

Akhilleus lives a powerful but short life, attaining Undying Glory: fame that lives on until men no longer populate the earth. With a choice between a long life and no glory and a short life with eternal glory, Akhilleus chooses the latter without a second's thought.

By looking at the Epic Cycle fragments as a whole, we can piece together the life of Akhilleus.

He is fathered by Peleus and born of the sea nymph Thetis. As an infant, Akhilleus' immortal mother attempts to destroy his mortal part by cooking him each evening over a fire. Peleus catches her doing this, and she leaves both her husband and son. As his mother's work is left unfinished, Akhilleus is not made immortal.

Peleus sends the boy to live with the centaur Kheiron, who raises him in the forested mountains on the marrow of wild animals. He absorbs the animals' essence, making him swift and powerful. Before the Trojan War breaks out, Thetis sends Akhilleus to Skyros, hiding him among the girls at Lykomedes' palace. Here he sires his son Phyrros (known as Neoptolemos) upon Deidaneia, daughter of King Lykomedes.

Odysseus plays a trick that reveals Akhilleus who, knowing his fate, decides to join the Akhaian campaign against Troy. He goes to Ilion and sacks many neighbouring cities, proving himself – though young – to be the best fighter. He also kills King Tenes (son of Apollon) on the island of Tenedos, as well as the Trojan child prince Troilos at the temple of Thymbrian Apollon, invoking the god's wrath.

In the ninth year, Apollon brings a plague on the Akhaians, and Agamemnon must return his war bride Kryseis, the daughter of Apollon's priest. At an assembly, Akhilleus provokes Agamemnon to anger, causing the Akhaian leader to take Akhilleus' prize, Briseis. Akhilleus withdraws from the war and his mother appeals to Zeus to make the Akhaians lose until her son returns to battle.

Eventually, Akhilleus' comrade Patroklos takes the elite Myrmidons out to meet the Trojans. He is slain by Hektor, the prince and champion of Troy. Akhilleus rejoins the battle and turns the tide.

He slays Hektor, and later the Aithiopian prince Memnon, son of Eos (Goddess of Dawn). Then he himself is slain by Apollon and Paris. He is given a grand funeral with games, and his cremated remains are buried with his comrades Patroklos and Antilokhos under an imposing tumulus.

The deepest insight we gain into Akhilleus is from the *Iliad*. It is the tale of his brief interlude from the battlefield of Ilion due to his anger caused by the actions of Agamemnon. The poem takes place over a few days towards the end of the war.

Akhilleus' absence from much of the poem heightens the scenes in which he appears, adding to their intensity. It is from these books of the *Iliad* we can draw out the ancestral lessons of the Greeks.

The Steppe Warrior

Akhilleus' frame of mind is that of the Steppe. He carries a pre-urban purity more than any other hero. He speaks the truth in a way others cannot.

Love and violence are bound together in his heart: love for his friend Patroklos, violence for his enemy Hector. Those who are close to him love him. Those who are far fear him, as they do the god Apollon.

Akhilleus is from the North, and his simple way conflicts with the complex Southern customs. His homeland of Phthia is farthest north of all heroes in the *Iliad*. It has never been placed in a historical location.

Akhilleus is half-divine with no identifiable city, and brought up by a centaur in the mountains. He is disconnected from the events at Troy. His story is both physically and psychologically removed.

When he receives Odysseus and the embassy from Agamemnon, he does so in a Steppe-appropriate manner. This is a hosting style that permeates Homer's works. Akhilleus offers his guests meat and will not hear of their mission until they have eaten and drunk with him (even though he has already concluded his own dinner).

The offer of gifts to make amends holds no sway over him. He rejects the inducements of Agamemnon, who seeks to yoke Akhilleus as a subordinate through the medium of material wealth. He derides ownership of objects and the desires of power, which are of no interest to a man of honour.

He labels Agamemnon "greediest, most possession-loving of men." Akhilleus sees him as reliant on his status and authority to take spoils he has not earned through battle. Akhilleus only wants to regain what was taken from him: his glory.

Akhilleus is an idealist – the embodiment of dignity above all. As a Steppe chieftain, he cannot accept an urbanised over-king like Agamemnon, even if offered gifts of the Steppe. Akhilleus states simply that "cattle and fat flocks can be stolen, tripods and red-maned horses can be won."

Akhilleus is not the only Steppe warrior in the *Iliad* by any means. All the Akhaians display traits of the Indo-European warrior band. Akhilleus, however, epitomizes the Steppe.

The closest hero to Akhilleus in the *Iliad* is Diomedes, who is also archetypal of the young wolf warrior. But neither he, nor the second best of the Akhaians (Aias), can replace Akhilleus in facing the Trojans. Only the pure fury of an unbridled Northern warrior can defeat the Trojans' best.

Akhilleus against Hektor is a clash between two distinct ways of life. Hektor means "defender of the city." Hektor is the city with its walls, battlements, and gates. He is the confined, crowded urban mass.

Akhilleus is the Steppe: the plain, flatlands, chariot, and horse – the bronze warrior, fire, the Dog Star. When Hektor meets Akhilleus in *monomakhía* ("individual combat"), it is on the plain outside the city wall. The city is Hektor's weakness, as all it contains is of high value to him; the plain is where Akhilleus is strong.

This is why the berserker wolfish state of *lússā* is so dangerous to Hektor, but not to the Apollo-like wolf-warrior Akhilleus. There is a thin line separating champion from berserk. Hektor crosses the line, whereas Akhilleus uses berserk traits while remaining a champion.

Hektor makes a fatal mistake. He departs as a member of the warrior band, becoming an unhinged lone wolf. He fights alone and for himself against Akhilleus, outside the proscriptive walls of Troy.

Even the more balanced warrior has issues functioning outside of a war context. With his berserk traits, Akhilleus cannot operate outside of the Trojan war. He cannot return to society.

Akhilleus can only function within the fraternal warrior band. It is governed by a collective *ēthos*, which denotes "self-law" and "autonomy." *Ēthos* is outside of societal law, and the wolf warrior band is self-governed through its own laws. Akhilleus is a perpetual wolf warrior, forever apart from society: a permanent outsider.

Akhilleus is the true Northern hero. He cannot and will not adapt to Southern ways. He cannot allow himself to be modernised, since it is against his essential nature.

As voice of the Northern past, Akhilleus reminds us we are wanderers – Cosmic nomads. This ancient truth survives through him into this world of cities, greed, decadence, and indifference. He remains pure in face of the Southern present and its ignobility.

Akhilleus cannot reconcile these two opposing ways of life. He has long time horizons; he seeks the eternal and is attuned to the Cosmic cycle. He takes in stride his dizzying relationship with death and fate.

Fate and Necessity

Akhilleus' name is linked to the verb *akakhizen*, meaning to grieve. It could literally translate as "he who has the host of fighting men grieving." Through both his absence and return, he brings the *pêma mégiston* ("greatest pain") to both sides during the war. He is a man of *mênis* (anger), of single-minded passion. Akhilleus also embodies *krátos* (superior power), the opposite of his eponymous *ákhos* (grief).

Akhilleus is *áristos Akhaiôn*: "best of the Akhaians." He is the most warlike, powerful, and dangerous on the battlefield; he is also filled with obstinacy and pride. Akhilleus is single-minded, set to an angry purpose. Bound by his doom he is swift of foot and of fate, fixed in rage and revenge.

Given the chance to stay home and live long without fame, or go to Troy and live short with fame, Akhilleus chooses the latter. While fate controls his future, he takes it into his own hands, making the decision between the two paths ahead of him for himself. He chooses to remain forever young and idealistic, to maintain a "great-spirited heart," which is quick to anger.

Being impetuous and having trouble restraining his temper, he needs guidance from his older companions Phoinix and Patroklos. This swift anger is what starts the wheel of fate in the *Iliad*. While a great warrior, Akhilleus is poor in the arts of peace; he does not understand the subtleties of diplomacy.

In the initial assembly at the beginning of the *Iliad*, Akhilleus is intelligent, but insensitive. He is too direct, speaking "straight." He sees the situation clearly, but has no empathy with Agamemnon. He cannot see things from another man's point of view.

While also a source of powerful rhetoric and greatness as a warrior, Akhilleus' clarity of vision makes him difficult to deal with. He acts and speaks without half-measures, which provokes Agamemnon to take away Akhilleus' war bride. This outrageous action in turn causes *khólos* (rage) in Akhilleus.

Akhilleus wishes to kill Agamemnon, which would be excusable under the circumstances in heroic society. Because his *géras* (prize) has been taken, his *tīmḗ* (honour) has been impugned and his *kûdos* (glory) diminished. Regardless whether he acts, reconciliation is unacceptable to Akhilleus.

Settling this dispute would mean the heroic community would be forced to side with the unjust Agamemnon, as he is leader. Thus, Akhilleus feels evicted from the heroic band. The attempt to bring him back into the fold through the embassy of Odysseus and Aias only leads him to feeling more isolated.

Akhilleus' exclusion from heroic society is an existential crisis. On one hand, by being pushed out of the culture he operates within, he is able to view it more critically from the outside – to self-examine and meditate on his place in heroic society. On the other, his anger leads him into an impossible situation.

Akhilleus cannot leave Troy and return to Phthia. He cannot escape his destiny, as he is already far enough along the path he chose. He is not of the domesticated, peaceful world. He cannot lose the honour and glory he has already accrued, but die nevertheless.

Akhilleus cannot choose reconciliation either, and can only return under compulsion: from *anánke* (absolute necessity). Akhilleus' refusal of a warrior role under the circumstances is an affirmation of true warrior ethics. It is this which makes him the purest hero. His absolutism, however, is disastrous and he is a victim of his own morality.

Since Akhilleus' honour will not allow him to leave, even though he threatens to, he makes an oath that he will not fight until Hektor comes to the camp of the Myrmidons. This places him in a situation that, even when he has digested his *khólos*, he cannot break his own vow not to fight. To circumvent this, he sends Patroklos out in his stead.

In combination with the turning of the wheel of fate, Akhilleus is also too open to suggestion. Phoinix suggests the vow, and Nestor suggests sending Patroklos. Neither of these are his own original ideas, but machinations of fate working through these elder advisors.

Patroklos' death brings new clarity to Akhilleus. His spirit is constrained by a new necessity: he has an absolute obligation to avenge his friend. Since Patroklos dies, Hektor must die, so Akhilleus must die; so all who fight Akhilleus must die.

Akhilleus is in the chain of *anánke*. Provoked to wrath, unable to accept the gifts, and forced to let Patroklos fight, he is finally made to rejoin the battle. The actions of Agamemnon cause Akhilleus to contemplate his fate, while Patroklos' death causes him to re-embrace it. After suffering he comes to a deeper understanding of the world, but only loss enables this.

When Hektor fights Akhilleus he wears Akhilleus' original set of divine armour. Akhilleus wears his new set, freshly forged by Hephaistos. Neither hero is invulnerable, but both are wearing invincible armour.

The men are pitted against each other on equal terms. The divine armour cannot prevent a ripening of the hero's fate, though he strives against time regardless. He sets forth to conquer by might, caring little for what fate allots him.

The thread of fate is woven throughout Akhilleus' time in Troy. Thetis tells Akhilleus not to kill Apollon's son Tenes, as Apollon will exact retribution; but he slays Tenes regardless. He does the same with Troilos, despite being forearmed with the knowledge of Apollon's wrath.

Akhilleus knows by killing Hektor he advances his fate further. Thetis warns him that killing Memnon will lead to his own death, but he ignores this also. On these occasions he knowingly embraces his fate, but does so on his own terms.

The chain of fatal events culminates with Akhilleus killing Memnon in battle, then attacking Troy. Through the agency of Apollon, Paris first shoots Akhilleus in the ankle. This impairs his legendary swiftness, as well as slowing his fate in the rush of battle.

The wound gives the hero pause to understand his death is imminent. Paris then fulfils fate and the will of Apollon by shooting Akhilleus with a deathly arrow.

Foresight of death is a divine capability. Akhilleus is the only hero of the Trojan Cycle with knowledge of his own death. Akhilleus is both mortal and immortal, but his death at Troy cannot be prevented, despite the efforts of his divine mother.

Akhilleus gains true immortality through his heroic actions. No god or goddess can grant immortality. This must be taken by the hero's own hand alone.

The hero knows he is fated to die fighting an equally powerful hero who defeats him. He is killed by a god and another hero; a battle rages over his corpse. A huge funeral and games are held, and he is made immortal after death.

Akhilleus is different from others in his greater capacity to deny, kill, refuse, and face death. He does not look back, but only lives in the now, looking forward. He does not dwell in the past once he has processed something.

Akhilleus has the ability and right to conceive his own law and put it into action. He, like the highest heroes, is a man of clarity and purity. He is able to will the impossible until making it possible.

Akhilleus is heroic, not demonic. This is because his negations are not founded on perversity of will, but clarity of intellect. He has both immediacy and an absolute lack of illusion.

Hektor, in contrast, is a man of illusions. He is a hero trapped between a failed connivance and his own incapacity for disenchantment.

Akhilleus is a superhuman figure. He has no proper place in the human world. He is the destroyer; he brings devastation on the Greeks, then the Trojans.

This is because he has no choice left in the chain of necessity to which he links himself. Throughout his *aristeíā* (battlefield excellence), he kills with both cold certainty and pure joy. The death of Patroklos unleashes a merciless Akhilleus on the Trojans.

Akhilleus fulfils himself in vivid experience of life; he accepts what it brings to him, including death. He is passionate and intelligent, impulsive and lucidly reflective. He expresses himself completely in his words and actions. He is totally known to his fellow heroes, with no hidden depths or clandestine motives.

Patroklos

Akhilleus' stubbornness leads to the death of Patroklos, his closest friend who was raised alongside him like a brother. Patroklos is the *therápōn* of Akhilleus. This word means retainer, or second in command, but carries a second meaning: "ritual substitute." Patroklos is Akhilleus' alter ego and his death foreshadows, yet postpones that of Akhilleus.

Apollon kills Patroklos because he is Akhilleus' *therápōn*, his substitute. Akhilleus is also a *therápōn* of Apollon. The gods experience death through the death of their *therápōn* – the hero dies on behalf of their god.

Patroklos is the mortal twin of the immortal Akhilleus. Patroklos means "he who has the glory of the ancestors." He represents the mortal ancestral line.

Upon the death of Akhilleus, the two are buried together in the same golden funerary urn given to Thetis at her wedding by the god Dionysos. This is a direct reflection of the Indo-European divine twins: one mortal and the other immortal, sharing both a tomb and immortality.

That the urn was given by Dionysos indicates the heroes will live an immortal Underworld existence after death. Dionysos is linked with the heroic dead who do not transcend beyond the gods. Instead, they remain in the heroic paradises of the Underworld, such as the Elysian Plain, Isles of the Blessed, and white island of Leuke.

After Akhilleus has avenged Patroklos and slain Hektor, he is already in the Underworld, since his mortal twin is dead.

When Priam sets out to retrieve Hektor's body from Akhilleus, he is conducted to him by Hermes, the psychopomp. Hermes meets Priam at the tomb of Ilos at sunset, then returns him to the tomb at sunrise. The two of them follow the sun into the Underworld and back.

Until the embassy of Priam, Akhilleus is savage and inflexible – he is pitiless. Once pity sets in with Akhilleus, he becomes a more refined hero. He fully understands his role, his fate and his place in the cosmos.

Apollon

Akhilleus is parallel to Apollon. Both are filled with *mênis* (anger) that inflicts *álgea* (pain) so as to be a *loigós* (devastation) for the Akhaians. Apollon has *mênis* about Kryseis' abduction by the Akhaians; Akhilleus has *mênis* about Bryseis' abduction by Agamemnon. Both inflict *álgea* on the Greeks because of this anger.

They are both represented as a *koûros* (youthful, unshorn, uninitiated male). They are doppelgängers. Akhilleus symbolises *bíē* (might).

Akhilleus is also as fast as the wind. Wind is a manifestation of *bíē*. Swiftness like the wind is the outward manifestation of Akhilleus' *bíē*.

160

Apollon is also associated with the wind in his role as Apollon Lykeios. This is the god of the *hybristes*; the youthful band of wolf warriors. Akhilleus is a *hybriste*, a wolf warrior who enters a rabid state of *lússā*, never destined to return to society.

Akhilleus has not yet cut his youthful locks and dedicated them to Apollon, as tradition dictated for those entering mature society. He has not subjugated himself to the god through initiation – he is still the wolf warrior. Instead, he has promised his hair to the local river god Sperkheios if he ever returns to his homeland Phthia. When he stands over the corpse of Patroklos, he cuts his locks and places them in the hands of his alter ego.

Akhilleus states directly he is in full opposition to Apollon. When he is tricked by the god, allowing the Trojans to escape within the city wall, Akhilleus says to Apollon's face that he would be revenged on him if he had the power.

The hostility of Apollon and Akhilleus has a religious dimension – they are ritual antagonists. Apollon needs to destroy Akhilleus so he does not supplant him. Initially, Zeus wanted to lie with Thetis, but was told that the progeny of that coupling would have become ruler of the Cosmos. Thus, Thetis was given to Peleus in marriage. Akhilleus still represents a threat to the genuine son of Zeus and inheritor of the Cosmic crown, Apollon.

As Apollon is Akhilleus' ritual antagonist, Athena is Hektor's. Hektor takes on the role of the spear-wielding protector of Troy, which is Athena's role as embodied in the Palladion statue. Athena and Apollon are Zeus' favourite children – they are the two highest gods in the Olympian hierarchy after the Thunderer himself.

Hektor replaces Athena as protector of Troy, so the goddess gives her aid to Akhilleus and the Akhaians. Akhilleus takes the role of leader of the youthful warrior band (the role of Apollon), causing the god to give his aid to Hektor, Paris, and the Trojans. Apollon gives Hektor the *kûdos*, emblem of victory, which is Akhilleus' armour taken from Patroklos. Akhilleus wins back the *kûdos* when he kills Hektor with the aid of Athena.

The gods strive against those who seek to supplant them. Having the characteristics of the gods is acceptable, but taking on their role entirely invokes their wrath. The gods do not want the hero to gain the same *tīmé* (honour) as them, contriving the death of those who seek to take what is theirs.

Aside from his relationship with Apollon, Akhilleus is only in conflict with men, not gods. Even when he is attacked by the Xanthos-Skamandros river, he does not fight back. When he realises he is tricked by Apollon, he does not try to fight him.

Akhilleus never loses confidence in the gods. He is part of the divine community. His mother is a goddess.

Akhilleus obeys the gods in the *Iliad* – Athena at the beginning when he does not kill Agamemnon, and Zeus at the end when he ransoms Hektor to Priam. This is because Akhilleus is a god among men. He has no place in the human community.

After his death, Akhilleus is embraced by Apollon, as he is placed in a subservient role to him. Akhilleus remains in an Apollon-like state on Leuke, the White Island of Apollon in the Hyperborean North. He becomes a true *therápōn* to the god in the heroic paradise, where he no longer represents a threat to Apollon's power.

Fire

Fire dominates the *Iliad*. It is the poem's emblem, and the symbol of Akhilleus. The metaphoric references to fire are the most numerous. The undertone of the poem begins with a kindling of fire as the wrath of Akhilleus.

The theme of fire continues to grow in intensity throughout the *Iliad*. It is hottest when Akhilleus rejoins the battle and ends with the funeral pyre of Patroklos. The fire is doused at Patroklos' funeral, as the anger of Akhilleus has abated. There are few references to fire after the funeral, though Hektor is cremated on the embers of Iliadic fire.

Cosmic fire marks the reentry of Akhilleus into battle. Athena brings about a *phlóx* ("flame") that burns over the hero's head. The Trojans are terrified by his *akámoton pyr* (inexhaustible fire). Once back on the battlefield, Akhilleus is no longer a leader of men, but a destroyer – a fire that sweeps through the Trojans.

Akhilleus running onto the plain appears to Priam like the autumn Dog Star, which is associated with fire. He becomes a fiery demon of death, dog of Orion, harbinger of the Trojan demise. He is the dog warrior, the wolf warrior.

His spear is compared to the fiery gleam of the evening star Phosphoros. This is the star of sunset. It leads the sun when it takes souls down to the Underworld.

Hephaistos hurls fire at the river Xanthos-Skamandros to free Akhilleus (fire defeats water). When he sees his new armour, Akhilleus' "eyes gleam like fire," and in battle his "hands gleam like consuming fire." Akhilleus in his bronze armour seems "like the light of a burning fire or the rising sun."

Fire is also associated with other heroes when they act as substitutes for Akhilleus. When Diomedes is in the midst of his *aristeía*, Athena causes him to appear as fire ("from his helmet she made blaze an unwearying flame"). Hektor also is associated with fire, but to a lesser extent; pitting his fire against water, he wishes to burn the Akhaian ships, but is unsuccessful.

Iliadic fire is *ménos* (inner fire). Fire is the symbol of Akhilleus – he is the man of *ménos*. Akhilleus burns with *ménos* and *mênis* (rage). Fire has dominion over earth and Akhilleus has power on the battlefield. Fire is the prime manifestation of *bíē* (might) on a cosmic level. Just as ritual fire causes the sun to rise, Akhilleus pulls himself from the darkness of despair through the inner fire of his might.

The internal fire of *ménos* is used by Akhilleus to burn away his mortality and refine his immortal Self. When he is finally cremated (after the events of the *Iliad*), his pyre achieves what his mother Thetis could not when he was an infant. In the Homeric hymn to Demeter, the goddess attempts to burn away the mortal part of the infant Demophoön in the same manner as Thetis. Fire is the key element to burn away mortality.

Akhilleus' apotheosis is similar to that of Herakles, with fire being the key to allowing him to attain immortality. The *eidôlon* is a shade of the mortal: the burned part that resides in the Underworld. After the mortal flesh and bone are burned off, a wholly immortal ascended body is translated to Olympos, or to the Northern heroic paradise on the White Island of Leuke.

The hero turns fire into light. The inner fire that he has kindled and fed burns his lower self, leaving only the pure being of light who is worthy of taking his place among the heroic dead.

The Solar Path

Akhilleus never truly returns to the human community, even after he is reconciled with Priam. He is not of the world, but a purer time. He is innocent in his idealism; this is what earns him his immortality.

Akhilleus is free of his community. This is contrasted by Hektor who remains in his community, subject to society.

Akhilleus is born of Thetis, a sea goddess. He is fire born of water, like the Vedic god Agni. He is a sun born of the sea.

The path of the sun is not the journey's entirety, but its horizontal section. Once the hero has emulated the sun by rising, setting, and rising once more, he must begin the vertical climb. Akhilleus completes the Solar Path, but ends his journey before the Polar Ascent.

Akhilleus is associated with the North mythologically. He gains Northern immortality only after death. As a substitute for Apollon, he gains the heroic immortality of the island of Leuke in the Far North.

Akhilleus achieves a liminal, posthumous immortality among the Apollonian people of Hyperborea. He is unable to go fully beyond the gods, remaining a *therápōn* of Apollon.

Akhilleus is killed by Apollon for attempted titanic usurpation of his role. He is brought under Apollon's dominion where he represents no threat to the Olympian order (much as Kronos continues to rule in a Golden Age over the Isles of the Blessed). He exists in a golden state on the edge of the Cosmos.

This paradise of the heroic dead is a place of horizontal transcendence. It only requires pure action, not the additional contemplative, psychonautic element that balances a hero. The lesser holy war must be complemented by a greater one against the lower self.

The outer must reflect the inner. To exist only in the realm of pure action can only bring about horizontal transcendence at best. This is what differentiates Solar and Polar mentalities.

Both Akhilleus and Diomedes are handed immortality by goddesses. Akhilleus is given it by Thetis, and Diomedes by Athena. They both go to the Isles of the Blessed, Elysion, or Leuke.

This is an Underworld immortality. The heroes who live on the Isles of the Blessed have achieved horizontal transcendence.

However, the hero who can transcend vertically escapes the material plane entirely. He goes beyond the gods to the *atidevic* state of *metátheos*. He exists outside the constructs of time and space.

The hero who can return to Hyperborea in his lifetime is able to go further. He must traverse the horizontal Solar Path, ritually dying and coming back to the land of the living, before travelling North on the Polar Ascent. Once he arrives at the Hyperborean state, he is able to reach beyond the gods to *metátheos-atideva*.

Part IV: The Return Journey

Ὀδυσεύς

Odysseus

Odysseus more than exemplifies the mature, seasoned hero. He goes beyond the role in his ingenuity combined with bravery. The first line of the *Odyssey* states that Odysseus is *polytrópos*. This has a dual meaning of both "very wily" and "much wandering." In one word, this describes both what the hero is and what he does.

Odysseus' name is linked to the words *odysao* ("I hate") and *odyssámenos* ("he who hates"). This pun is played on a lot in the *Odyssey*. Given him by his maternal grandfather Autolykos, the name could mean "he who is hated." It is also connected to the words *odyrómenos* ("he who laments") and *odýnē* (pain/suffering). This is an apt name for a man whose tale is one of wandering through a strange world while suffering the consequences of bringing the hatred of Poseidon upon himself.

The first epithet he is given in the *Odyssey* is *antítheos*. This is used to mean "godlike," but carries a second meaning: "god-opposed." He is set in opposition to Poseidon and Helios, but ultimately against all the gods as he strives to reach beyond them. This state "beyond the gods" is called *metátheos* (*atideva* in Sanskrit).

Poseidon is an older god, the pre-Olympian Earth Shaker. He once held the most important role in the pre-Greek religion. His name means "bridegroom," and his original function is husband of the Earth Mother.

Helios is the Titanic sun. Odysseus embodies the Olympian spirit – the golden streak of the heroic. He must appease the older gods at the end of his journey and reconcile with them.

Odysseus is *tlētós* (enduring) and *streptós* (flexible). He is gritty and able to endure the toughest of hardships. In the *Odyssey* he says to the nymph Kalypso, "Though some god may wreck me again on the wine-dark deep, I will endure: the heart in my breast can bear much trouble! Before now I have suffered much, have laboured greatly amid waves and in warfare: to all that let this be added."

Odysseus also says he is "made weak by time and fate, but strong in mind to strive, to seek, and not to yield."

He is, however, capable of bending; of changing his plans based on the scenario he finds himself in. Odysseus embodies *mêtis*: many-faced planning. He has a strategy for any situation and can employ it appropriately.

Odysseus uses words and actions with balance. He is versatile and meets each challenge in the suitable manner. He deals with witches and princesses, adapting and showing his flexibility. He is wily, tactful, ingenious, charming, and formidable in equal measure.

Odysseus' vagaries leave him more himself than ever. He oscillates between states of Being, never entering a state of becoming. He does not change through his journey. He is the same man from the outset of the *Iliad* until the end of the *Odyssey*. He is wiser for the journey and hides his genuine nature from many, but his true Self remains unchanging.

Odysseus is fully developed, but continually learning. Only after a man is fully developed can he truly learn. He can either change as a person or grow wiser in himself, but not both.

Odysseus embodies obscured truth. His two-faced soul confronts the outer world with steadfast daring, and the inner one with poetic vision. He is immovable, sanguine in his depths when faced with disaster.

Odysseus is gentle to friends and family, yet unforgiving to enemies. A Divine King, he is father to his people.

Having visited the Underworld, Odysseus is "twice-dead when other men die." He also introduces himself succinctly in the Phaiakian court: "I am Odysseus son of Lairtes, who plies all manner of wiles among men, and my fame reaches heaven."

Like that of Akhilleus, the story of Odysseus as laid out in the Epic Cycle fragments can be pieced together to make a single narrative.

Odysseus is the legitimate born child of Lairtes, king of Ithake and Kephalonia, and his queen Antiklea. Lairtes was an Argonaut and participated in the Kalydonian Boar Hunt. As a youth, Odysseus visits his maternal grandfather Autolykos (son of the god Hermes) on Mount Parnassos – holy mountain of Apollon. He hunts a boar, receiving a scar from the beast when it gores him, then returns to Ithake an initiated adult.

When the chieftains of Greece all assemble to court Helen in the palace of Tyndareos, Odysseus helps the king by suggesting the suitors all swear an oath to protect the rights of whoever is successful. He asks in return that he can marry Penelope, daughter of Ikarios (Tyndareos' brother). Odysseus marries Penelope, taking over the rule of his father's kingdom and allowing Lairtes to retire.

He sires his son Telemakhos; and while he is still an infant, Menelaos, Agamemnon, Nestor, and Palamedes arrive to enforce the Oath of Tyndareos and enlist him to fight in the Trojan War. Wishing to stay out of the conflict, Odysseus feigns insanity by yoking a donkey and an ox to a plough, sowing salt.

Palamedes calls Odysseus' bluff and places Telemakhos in the path of the plough. Odysseus stops the plough and saves his son, revealing his sanity. For this, he maintains a grudge against Palamedes.

Odysseus joins the war effort, helping the Akhaians enlist Akhilleus before they all head to Troy. Often fighting alongside Diomedes, Odysseus proves himself a powerful warrior. He and Diomedes eventually take revenge on Palamedes during a mission by drowning him in the sea.

Odysseus has the responsibility of taking charge of missions requiring tact and intelligence. He is chosen to be part of the embassy to Akhilleus in the *Iliad.* He likewise goes on a night mission with Diomedes in which they kill the Thracian king.

When Akhilleus is killed by Paris, Odysseus and Aias rescue the corpse, bringing it back to the Akhaian camp. At the funeral of Akhilleus, the Trojan captives name Odysseus the more damaging hero to the Trojan cause, winning him the armour of Akhilleus. Having lost the contest, Aias goes mad and kills the cattle of the Akhaians, then himself.

Odysseus captures the Trojan prince Helenos, who, angered by the Trojans, joins the Akhaian cause. Helenos prophesies the conditions needed for Troy to fall. Odysseus and Diomedes then go to fetch Akhilleus' son Neoptolemos, as well as the archer

Philoktetes, both of whom are necessary for the Akhaians to win the war. The pair then enter Troy at night on a stealth mission and steal the Palladion statue from the city, fulfilling another condition for the city's fall.

Athena inspires Epeios to build the wooden horse, and Odysseus is instrumental in the planning and execution of the tactic. Odysseus disguises himself and enters Troy. He meets with Helen and discusses the impending sacking, before fleeing the city and killing several Trojans on the way out. He is one of the elite heroes in the horse.

After the sack of Troy, Odysseus begins his journey home. He sacks the city of the Kikonians, visits the land of the Lotus Eaters, blinds the kyklops, and almost makes it home to Ithake with the help of Aiolos' bag of winds, but is thwarted by his inquisitive crew. He loses all but his own ship in the land of the Laistrygonians, then stays with the sorceress Kirke for a year before visiting the seer Teiresias in the Underworld. After passing the Sirens and the monster Skylla, he is stranded on Thrinakia, where his crew eat some of the Cattle of Helios, leading to their downfall.

Leaving Thrinakia, Zeus wrecks the ship on behalf of his brother Poseidon, killing all but Odysseus, who escapes death by the whirlpool of Kharybdis. He is washed up to the nymph Kalypso's island and stranded for seven years. Kalypso treats him like a husband, but Odysseus dreams of returning to Ithake.

Athena intercedes on his behalf, requesting Zeus help him return home. Zeus sends Hermes to instruct Kalypso to release the hero. Odysseus builds a raft, setting sail. Poseidon notices him on his way home and wrecks him near Phaiakia. The Phaiakians help Odysseus, transporting him back to Ithake.

Disguised as a beggar, he infiltrates his palace. With the help of his son and loyal servants, he kills the suitors who are wooing his wife Penelope after his twenty-year absence.

Odysseus then leaves Ithake to complete the rites proscribed by Teiresias. He first goes to Elis to visit his herds, before heading north to the Sacred Oak of Zeus at Dodona. There, he learns he will be killed by his own son.

Odysseus continues north until he reaches the land of the Thesprotians, who have no contact with the sea. He performs the sacrifice to Poseidon and is welcomed into the Thesprotian court. He marries the queen Kallidike, siring a son: Polypoites.

He fends off the neighbouring Brygoi tribe, who are assisted by Ares. With the help of Athena he repels their attack, but this fight between deities and tribes is broken up by Apollon. After several years, Kallidike dies and Polypoites becomes king.

Odysseus returns to Ithake. In his absence, his second son by Penelope, Polyporthes, has been born and grown into a youth.

When he was with Kirke, Odysseus sired a son with her called Telegonos. This unknown son searches for his father and arrives on Ithake, where he begins to ravage the land. Odysseus goes out to fight the stranger and is slain by Telegonos' poisoned stingray barb spear, giving him the gentle death from the sea foreseen by Teiresias.

Telegonos realises that he has killed his father and, aided by Telemakhos and Penelope, takes his corpse to Kirke's island for cremation. Kirke bestows immortality on the trio and marries Telemakhos, while Penelope marries Telegonos. Polyporthes remains on Ithake as king.

Ὀδυσεύς της ιλιάδας

Odysseus of the *Iliad*

The *Iliad* and *Odyssey* are two main sources from which we can gain a true insight into Odysseus and his nature. He is the same man in both epics, but his circumstances are different in each.

In the *Iliad* his position is as a clever leader of many and respected adviser. While a free spirit in his inner life, he is a conservative force of order, balance, and tradition – a preserver of hierarchy. When the mob raises its ugly head in the speech of Thersites, Odysseus beats the soldier severely. He says that there will be no leadership from the multitude: there can be only one ruler.

He, along with Nestor, is always on the side of Agamemnon; not because of personal loyalty, but due to his respect for the correct hierarchy. Agamemnon is leader due to his status. Despite his shortcomings, Odysseus works to preserve Agamemnon's position while correcting his mistakes. He is an agent of order.

Odysseus' value as a reliable diplomat – a steady hand who is friendly across the generations – puts him in a position of great trust and respect. He is often chosen as an ambassador and negotiator. He is sent on missions, usually accompanied by his younger accomplice Diomedes.

Diomedes

Throughout the *Iliad*, Diomedes is always at Odysseus' side. Other parts of the Epic Cycle reflect this, and the two form an inseparable pair. His name suggests he is a counterpart of Odysseus, since it means "godlike cunning," or "advised by Zeus." *Mêtis* (artifice and strategy) is a quality embodied by Odysseus, and his younger comrade's name reflects this.

Like the relationship of Akhilleus and Patroklos, that of Odysseus and Diomedes is a reflection of the divine twin mythos. Diomedes is the pure warrior, and is given immortality by Athena upon his death after his exile from Argos, when he returns from Troy. Both Odysseus and Diomedes are loved and protected by Athena; both men return home, as does the other man associated with Odysseus: Nestor.

The connection between these two heroes and the Indo-European twin mythos is marked out in the Doloneia section of the *Iliad*. This part of the *Iliad* deals with the night mission, where

Odysseus and Diomedes meet the Trojan scout Dolon, extracting information from him and then killing him. The deeper mythological part of the Doloneia is when, following their meeting with Dolon, Odysseus and Diomedes enter the Thracian camp, slaying the Thracian king Rhesos and stealing his horses.

In Thrace, Rhesos was a cave daimon. The sun in Indo-European mythos goes to his cave each night before emerging each morning. Odysseus and Diomedes steal the horses of the Titanic sun.

This is the same as the Indo-European theft of the cattle of the sun. It is again echoed in the *Odyssey* when Odysseus steals the sheep of the kyklops. There is also a connection with Nestor, as the older hero's mythos has a story where he steals the cattle of the sun as well.

Diomedes and Nestor are likewise placed together in the *Iliad*. Nestor is under attack in book eight; seeing that the gods are against them, Odysseus retreats. Diomedes rescues Nestor, and then tries to press on. However, Nestor tells Diomedes that Zeus will not favour them, relaying to the young warrior what Odysseus already sees.

Diomedes is half of Odysseus, representing youthful arrogance that is powerful, but not always useful. Diomedes cannot completely see the hidden truths, aside from the brief period that Athena imparts the Olympian Stare upon him so he can battle the gods. He is the warlike part of the mature hero, which is let go of in Troy in order to embark on a Hermetic journey through the Underworld.

Aias

In the *Iliad*, Aias and Odysseus are also close comrades. They fight together. They both go on the embassy to Akhilleus to try and convince him to rejoin the war.

After the events of the *Iliad*, Aias and Odysseus rescue the body of Akhilleus together. In contrast to Odysseus, Aias represents the opposite end of the heroic spectrum. He has few, but straight words, compared to the well-spoken and intelligent Odysseus.

Aias is physically powerful, but emotionally fragile. This is brought to a head following the funeral games of Akhilleus in the *Aithiopis*. When Aias cannot take the slight of losing to Odysseus, he goes mad and kills himself.

In the *Odyssey*, the two appear before each other in the Underworld. However, Aias cannot bring himself to forgive Odysseus. The true hero must have mental fortitude as well as physical prowess.

Akhilleus

Akhilleus and Odysseus are also contrasted in the *Iliad*.

Unlike Akhilleus, Odysseus does not exhibit berserk traits. He is a champion and warrior who can function within society outside of a war context. He has the wide range of skills and social tools to be able to operate in a variety of settings.

During the embassy, before they eat, Akhilleus chooses to sit opposite Odysseus specifically. This shows the balance of the two heroes' attributes. Odysseus is a man of *mêtis* (strategy) and *nóos* (perception), while Akhilleus is a man of *mênos* (inner fire) and *bíē* (might).

Both are *āristos* ("best") in their fields of warfare and strategy. Akhilleus is simple and direct, Odysseus complex and convoluted. The fully realised hero must have both *bíē* and *mêtis*, *ménos* and *nóos*.

The Epic Cycle also reminds us that Odysseus, not Akhilleus, is destroyer of Troy. He does this through his *mêtis*.

Ὀδυσεύς της Ὀδύσσειας

Odysseus of the *Odyssey*

The circumstances of the *Odyssey* oppose those of the *Iliad*. Even before he loses his comrades, Odysseus wanders through another world, adrift at sea and alone. His tale shows us his true inner and outer nature.

Time and again Odysseus is shown to embody the epithet *polytropós* ("man of many twists and turns"). He is a man of many deceits, many ways. He is an ingenious trickster – a singular hero who fights against his fate.

The sea wandering of Odysseus brings him knowledge and meaning. He values this knowledge over material goods. There is nothing of material value in the places he visits.

Odysseus suffers but does not buckle, and bends when pushed but bends back. He is resolute, fierce, destructive, clever, funny, and loving. He has been everywhere, seen everything, thought of everything, invented everything, changed everything.

Odysseus interacts in person with supernatural beings, and can perceive the gods when they are before him. Odysseus' voyage is internal; it is a journey of the Spirit.

Nóstos

Odysseus' return from Troy to his homeland of Ithake is a journey through both the Underworld and the mind. The key to understanding this is the Indo-European root syllable *nes-*. This syllable is the root of the Greek words *néomai* ("return home"), *nóstos* ("return") and *nóos* (perception).

Nes- is also at the root of the Vedic name *Nāsatyau*, an epithet of the divine twins who bring mortals back to life. *Nes-* means "return from death and darkness," and therefore also "return to life and light." Helios is agent of the demise of Odysseus' men, and the journey of the Titanic sun into the Underworld and back is reflected in the hero's journey. Odysseus returns home to the light from the darkness; his return is from death to life.

Nóos is the key to *nóstos*, and both words dominate the *Odyssey*. *Nóos* as mental-spiritual "seeing" is related to consciousness, and brings about a return from death. At the opening of the *Odyssey*, Zeus says Odysseus "surpasses all other mortals in his *nóos*." He makes his return, while Odysseus' companions lose their *nóstos* due to their lack of *nóos*.

The importance of *nóos* in the *Odyssey* is heightened by the presence of Nestor: "The Returner." Nestor is the personification of *nóos*. In the *Iliad*, he comes to the fore whenever council is needed.

Nestor, not his advice, is the symbol of *nóos*. His presence indicates the presence of *nóos*. This is why it is speeches made by others (especially Odysseus) that contain actual council and advice.

The connection between Nestor and Odysseus is made clear throughout the *Iliad*. When Phoinix, Aias, and Odysseus go as embassy to Akhilleus, Nestor looks Odysseus in the eye longer than the other two, relaying an unspoken message to him. In the *Odyssey* his role is yet again simply to be there, showing the audience the presence of *nóos*.

Nestor has survived the passing of two generations in the Homeric works. He is an immortal from an ancient time. Nestor has already gone through the trials of death and return.

Nestor's original function in his own mythos was to release the cattle of the sun from the cave. He is like the Vedic Indra. The theft of cattle from the cave is the theft of light from darkness.

As a youth, Nestor raided the cattle of Augeias, son of Helios. Raiding the cattle of the sun from the cave of sunset is a return from death. This is why Nestor is the king of Pylos.

Pylos means "gate." The word was directly associated with the gates of the Underworld in Greek myth. Nestor, therefore, is associated with restoring mortals to life and light.

Nóos is necessary in order to fulfil *nóstos*, and Nestor is symbolic of both. This is his function in the Odyssey. Before we hear of what has become of Odysseus, we encounter Nestor through the travels of Telemakhos.

To the returner, the dark night of danger gives way to the daylight of victory. This is the rebirth from the ritual Solar Death. One who has been caught by actual death cannot return to life.

Sleep and death are intrinsically linked in ancient Greek thought. They are personified by the brothers Hypnos and Thanatos. On several occasions in the *Odyssey*, Odysseus falls asleep at inopportune times. This sleep of Odysseus marks his passing through death unharmed.

The sun represents the waking consciousness, and sleep puts the hero outside the influence of the sun. Sleep is not on the mortal plain, but beyond ordinary consciousness. As it sets, the sun begins a journey through the underworld, taking the souls of men with it. Only the privileged elect can pass through death unharmed; they do this by entering the dream world.

These *chrēmatismós* (divine dreams) only appear to *āristoi*. When a man becomes a true hero, the gods speak to him. He becomes a pontifex: bridge to the other world – a divine ruler.

Odysseus' journey home is a journey through the Underworld and *nóos*. It passes through the dreamworld of the elect in order to reach the point of ascent. It is a journey across "the unharvestable sea" – place of death, accompanied by "aláomai" (sailors, vagabonds, and the wandering dead).

This is the Solar Path of ritual death and rebirth bringing one to the foot of the Cosmic Mountain. The hero can attempt to make the vertical Polar Ascent only after completing this horizontal Solar transcendence.

Between leaving Troy and returning to Ithake, Odysseus must pass twelve barriers. These twelve *âthloi* (labours) are like those of Herakles, the earlier hero who completes the Solar Path. These twelve adventures take Odysseus from the liminal world, through the Underworld, and back.

In order, they are:

1. The Kikonians in Thrace
2. Land of the Lotus Eaters
3. The Kyklops
4. Aiolia, Land of the wind keeper Aiolos
5. Telepylos, Land of the Laistrygonians

6. Kirke on Aiaia

7. The Nékyia

8. The Sirens

9. Skylla and Kharybdis

10. Thrinakia and the Herds of Helios

11. Kalypso on Ogygia

12. Skheria, Land of the Phaiakians

Kikonians and Lotus Land

After setting sail from Troy, Odysseus and his twelve ships arrive at the city of the Kikonians (Ismaros in Thrace). The Akhaians sack the city, making off with treasure, cattle, and women. Odysseus is given the Ismarian wine by Maro, a priest of Apollon, in return for his protection of the sanctuary of the god. This is a secret, heavenly wine that is both potent and delicious.

As they are ready to depart, some of the men decide to slaughter cattle and feast on the shore. Odysseus advises against this, but is ignored. In the meantime, the Kikonians enlist the help of their allies and attack the men on the beach. The Greeks escape, but six men from each ship are killed by the Kikonians.

The decision to stay is a rash act of foolishness. The men are slain as they lack *nóos*. This is why they lose their return.

The ships are driven south to Kythera, and then again to Lotus Land. In a characteristic act of curiosity, Odysseus sends three men to discover what kind of people live there. They come upon the Lotus Eaters.

These people eat the mysterious lotus fruit, making them forget their purpose. The three crew members eat and forget themselves. They are dragged back to the ships on Odysseus' orders before setting sail.

Lotus Land is a place of oblivion; it is part of the Underworld, and its inhabitants are like shades of the dead who have lost their *nóos*. Odysseus' men "forget their return," but he retains his *nóos* (his memory) while in the Underworld.

In the realm of the dead, two springs are available to quench the thirst of the newly dead: *Léthē* (Spring of Forgetfulness) and *Mnemosýne* (Spring of Memory). Only the elect know to drink from the Spring of Memory and retain their *nóos*. A loss of memory results in a loss of return; retaining and reawakening memory allows the hero to return to the light.

Kyklops

Odysseus and his fleet next come to the land of the kyklopes. He keeps all but his personal ship harboured on a neighbouring island while investigating the island inhabited by the kyklopes.

He and twelve men find a cave with a flock of sheep inside. They sacrifice one of them and eat while awaiting the return of the cave's inhabitant, hoping for the usual Greek guest-friendship to be extended to them.

A giant man with one eye returns, bringing the rest of his flocks with him. He rolls a huge stone over the mouth of the cave, milks his sheep, and makes cheese. He then acknowledges the men before telling Odysseus he doesn't care about the laws of Zeus. Named Polyphemos, the kyklops picks up two of the men and dashes their brains out, eating them raw.

Odysseus realises if they simply kill Polyphemos, they will be trapped in the cave behind the giant rock. He must come up with a trick to escape. The next morning, the kyklops eats two more men before heading out. Odysseus finds a huge staff of olive wood and sets about sharpening the end, hardening it in the fire before hiding it under dung.

The kyklops returns and eats another two men. Odysseus engages him in conversation, offering the kyklops the strong Ismarian wine he has brought. Polyphemos gets drunk and asks Odysseus' name, to which the hero replies, "*Oûtis*," meaning "Nobody."

The kyklops passes out and the men drive the sharpened stake into his eye, blinding him. Polyphemos cries out in pain; when the neighbouring kyklopes shout out, asking what is wrong, Polyphemos says, "Nobody is killing me by trickery!" The other kyklopes do not investigate further.

The next morning, Polyphemos rolls the stone away and lets his sheep out, not knowing that Odysseus has strapped his men underneath them. They make their escape, and a jubilant Odysseus cannot help but shout out that he who blinded the kyklops is "Odysseus, sacker of cities ... the son of Lairtes, having a home in Ithake." The kyklops then cries out to his father Poseidon for revenge, bringing the wrath of the god onto Odysseus.

This story is that of the theft of the cattle and flocks of the sun from the cave of sunset. Kyklops means "Circle Eye." It is the wheel of the sun. Kyklops is the name of the Titanic sun himself. This is why the kyklops has only one eye – it is the eye of the sun.

The sun enters the cave at night with his flocks. The kyklops is the sun with his cattle in the cave of sunset. He represents the sunset aspect of the sun, taking souls down to the Underworld. Odysseus takes some of the sheep with him after escaping as he is on the cattle raid, stealing the flocks of the sun.

In his curiosity, Odysseus wishes to see the man who lives in the cave. He takes twelve men and the wineskin with him. Odysseus' continuous curiosity and desire to test himself comes to the fore again.

Twelve is a number associated with the sun and its journey through the zodiac. The number is reflected also in the total number of trials of Odysseus, and the number of ships he starts with. Half the men are killed, reflecting the six men from each ship killed by the Kikonians.

Odysseus has a foreboding of meeting a being with no judgement or customs, and enters the cave knowing that danger awaits him and his men. As expected, Polyphemos breaks the laws of Zeus when he eats his guests. Zeus Xenios is nothing to a son of Poseidon.

Odysseus uses *nóos* to escape the fate of the other men. *Oûtis* and *mêtis* (strategy) can both mean nobody in wordplay. The prefixes *ou* and *me* are both used to mean "no" in Homeric Greek.

Odysseus tells the kyklops he is "nobody," and that he is *"mêtis."* He tells the kyklops who he truly is. When regaling the Phaiakians with the story he says, "My own heart laughed at how my name and perfect design (*mêtis*) had fooled him."

In the kyklops' cave, the realm of the dead, he is *Oûtis* – anonymous like an *eidôlon* (shade of the dead). Once he leaves, he becomes Odysseus once again. He leaves the Underworld cave and remembers who he is: "Odysseus, sacker of cities … the son of Lairtes, having a home in Ithake."

Odysseus is concerned with his fame. He cannot resist shouting his real name after he escapes. He wants his deed attributed to his name.

Odysseus incurs the wrath of the sun, who invokes Poseidon to act as his proxy. Poseidon is agent of the Titanic sun's vengeance against a hero who strives to defeat the gods.

Aiolia and Laistrygonians

Odysseus arrives on Aiolia (Squall Island), home of Aiolos (Blower). This immortal is in charge of all of the winds. He offers the men a month's hospitality behind his bronze walls. Before Odysseus heads out, Aiolos gives him a bag that contains all the contrary winds, trapping them until they arrive on Ithake.

After ten days on watch, Odysseus falls asleep. His men, believing it to contain a treasure, open the bag, letting out the winds and sending them back to Aiolia. Aiolos is angered at their return and refuses to help for a second time a man "hated by the gods." The ships sail off after Aiolos tells them to leave.

Wind has dominion over water and Odysseus uses it on the sea. However, he is not able to make an easy return. As he has further trials to undertake, he loses the power of the winds.

Because Odysseus strives against the gods, he is hated. In this other world though, he is outside Olympian influence. Only the all-seeing Titanic sun, chthonic Earth Shaker Poseidon, and psychopomp Hermes are able to enter and operate in this realm. His patroness Athena is unable to assist him.

After seven days, the winds drive the ships to the land of the Laistrygonians in the far north, where the nights are short and herding is good. The Laistrygonians (Rough Pelts) live in almost perpetual daylight and have plentiful cattle and sheep. They are sociable among their own, but cannibalistic to outsiders.

The ships moor in the harbour of the Laistrygonians, but Odysseus keeps his ship anchored further away, outside the harbour. He sends two men and a herald to scout. They come upon a princess who takes them to the city of Telepylos, where they meet the huge queen of the Laistrygonians. She calls her husband Antiphates, who eats one of the men.

The other two retreat to tell Odysseus. The Laistrygonians then throw boulders at the ships in the harbour and spear the men like fish. Odysseus and the crew of his ship escape.

The Laistrygonians live in the city of Telepylos ("Far Gate"), the place where the sun both rises and sets. This is the entrance to the Underworld: Gate of the Sun. It is the cave at the ends of the earth where Underworldly shepherds meet and herd the cattle and flocks of the sun.

When his men meet the Laistrygonian queen they shrink in fear, as she is the Queen of the Underworld. Only Odysseus keeps his ship out of the Laistrygonian harbour, showing *nóos*. He passes through another Underworld trial while the other ships are lost.

Kirke

The solitary ship lands on Aiaia, island of the nymph Kirke (a daughter of Helios). After three days, Odysseus sees smoke and decides to investigate. First, he feasts the men on a huge stag he hunts, then admits to them that he has no idea where they are, as he cannot tell east from west. He sends Eurylokhos and half the men to investigate.

The scouting party are encircled by wolves and lions, who act as if domesticated. Kirke appears to them and brings them into her house, where she feeds them a kykeion (posset of wine, honey, onion, cheese, and barley) laced with a drug. Aside from Eurylokhos, who refrained from entering the house, the men are all turned into pigs.

Eurylokhos tells Odysseus, who arms himself and seeks out the witch. On his way, Hermes Argeïphontes appears to Odysseus. He gives Odysseus the moly plant antidote to the drugs of Kirke, as well as instructions on how to subdue her.

Odysseus is fed by Kirke, but does not transform. He draws his sword on her and threatens to kill her. The sorceress exclaims, "Surely you are Odysseus, the multifarious!"

Kirke then asks him to join her in bed. Odysseus first makes her swear an oath she will change his men back and not harm any of them. This she does, and Odysseus and his men are entertained by the nymph for a year.

After a year, Odysseus' men tell him to remember his fatherland and set sail for Ithake. Kirke informs him that he must consult the seer Teiresias in the realm of the dead. She tells Odysseus to sacrifice a black ram and ewe to the "glorious tribes of the dead," giving him directions to go to the doorway of the House of Hades.

One of Odysseus' men, Elpenor, wakes up after sleeping on the roof. Forgetting where he is, he falls to his death. The ship sails as the sun sets.

Kirke is daughter of the Titanic sun, Helios. This is reflected in her name, which means "Encircler" or "Circling Hawk" – describing attributes of the sun. She is a nymph: an intensely female sexual fairy or lower goddess. Nymph means "bride," which is what the sanskrit term *Śakti* can also mean. She is a pure feminine force – a sexual witch.

She dwells on the island Aiaia, which is also gateway of the sun into the Underworld. Odysseus does not know which is east and west; he cannot tell where the sun rises and sets. Kirke's island of Aiaia is in both East and West. Her name denotes the sun's path and its fluctuating position between East and West.

Kirke turns Odysseus' men into pigs. They are the preferred animal for sacrifices to Underworld deities. But due to the moly plant, the Encircler cannot turn the man of many turns.

Hermes, psychopomp (guide of souls), is great-grandfather of Odysseus. He gives him aid as no other god can in the Underworld, since Olympians do not enter it. The root of the moly is black and the flower is white – Hermes gives Odysseus the knowledge required to pass through darkness into light.

With his sword drawn against Kirke, he shows his indomitable spirit. Sex and food are taken on his terms. He outwits Kirke because, unlike his men, he retains his *nóos*.

Odysseus' men glut themselves while he exercises restraint, enjoying the delights of Kirke as master of the house. Hence, they are turned into pigs and he is not. Like the Underworld spring of *Léthē*, Kirke's drugs make the men forget their fatherland.

They stay a year, a full solar cycle, before the crew ask Odysseus to remember. The memory of life and light allows

Odysseus to pass through the Underworld. His retention of his *nóos* differentiates him from his men once more.

Elpenor is foolish. Falling from the roof, he loses his return. His lack of *nóos* prevents his *nóstos*. This happens at sunset when the sun takes souls to the Underworld.

Kirke sends Odysseus to the Underworld with the setting sun. Upon his return, she receives him back with the rising sun. This is the solar journey to the Underworld within the greater solar journey to the Underworld, which starts when Odysseus leaves Troy and ends when he returns to Ithake.

Nékyia

To journey to the Underworld, Odysseus sails north through the land of the Kimmerians – place of the long night, darkness, and death. He rides a north wind across Okeanos to a grove of poplars and willows outside the entrance to the House of Hades. Once there, the shades of the dead begin to come out of the mists of *Érebos* (murk of the Underworld). He then slaughters the black ram and ewe, collecting their blood in a pit; this is the *nékyia*, a necromantic rite to question the dead.

He keeps all the shades away with his sword until the Theban seer Teiresias approaches the blood and drinks. Upon questioning by Odysseus, Teiresias offers his prophesy:

"Great Odysseus, you want to know all about your sweet homecoming. This a god will make hard for you: I do not foresee you escaping the Earth Shaker's notice. He holds a grudge because you blinded his dear son.

"Yet even so you can make it, though after much hardship, if you are willing to curb your own and your comrade's spirits from the moment you put in with your well-built ship, forsaking the violet deep, to the isle of Thrinakia and find there at pasture the cattle and well-fed sheep of Helios, the all-seeing, all-hearing sun.

"If you leave these unharmed and take care over your return you may still get home to Ithake, after much suffering; but should you harm them, then I foresee destruction for your ship and your comrades. You yourself may escape, but you'll get home late and in bad shape, your comrades all lost, in a ship not your own, find troubles plaguing your house – arrogant fellows installed there, devouring your livelihood, wooing your godlike wife and sending her bridal gifts!

"Indeed, when you come you'll avenge their violent conduct, but when you've killed off the suitors in your halls, whether by guile or openly with the sharp bronze, then you must set out again, taking a well-planed oar, until you come among men who know nothing of the sea, who eat their food without putting salt in it, and have never set eyes on ships with purple cheeks or on the well-shaped oars that serve as a ship's wings; and I'll tell you a very clear sign, one that won't escape you: when on the road you meet another man who believes it's a

winnowing-fan that you have on your sturdy shoulder, then fix your
well-shaped oar on end in the ground, and offer a lavish sacrifice to the
lord Poseidon – a ram, a bull, and a stud boar that mounts its sows.

"Then go back home and make rich and sacred offerings to the
immortal gods who possess broad heaven, in due order. Death will come
to you from the sea, the gentlest of ends, but will take you only after
you've worn out a sleek old age, with your people around you
prospering.

"This that I tell you is the truth."

Odysseus lingers on well after his questioning of Teiresias is
over. He is curious to talk to all of the great dead and learn from
them. He first sees all the famous queens and women, including
his mother who has died while he was in Troy.

Odysseus then sees all his fallen comrades, learning from
Agamemnon the fate which has befallen him. He talks with
Akhilleus, discussing death and glory. He also sees the shade of
Elpenor who fell from the roof. The ghost tells him to give him
funeral rites, and place his oar upright in the earth as a marker.

After questioning the dead for a long time, Odysseus returns
to his ship and sails back to Kirke, landing at sunrise. Kirke says
that he is now "twice-dead," while others only die once. She then
gives him the directions on how to sail to Ithake, telling him
about the trials awaiting him.

Odysseus arrives at the grove by the entrance to the Underworld. He makes a *Haimakouría* (blood sacrifice) as part of the *nékyia*. The *nékyia* is not a *katábasis* (descent into the Underworld), but his entire voyage through the otherworld is.

Teiresias is one of the only shades to retain his *nóos* in the Underworld; he drinks the blood to gain pseudo-*ménos*, as the dead do not have the inner fire of the living. The blood reanimates the ghost. Teiresias does not give Odysseus directions to Ithake, but a warning about the Cattle of Helios and then instructions on where to go after he reaches Ithake.

Odysseus gains *nóos* from the *nékyia*. Retaining *nóos* is what separates the living and the dead. It is a prerequisite for journeying into darkness and death, then returning to light and life.

Odysseus gains knowledge and insight by questioning the dead. He discovers their secrets, the secrets of all the Greeks. The hero must face death, going to the place of death and confronting it in order to find answers.

When Akhilleus speaks to Odysseus, the dead hero of the *Iliad* speaks with the living hero of the *Odyssey*. Akhilleus gives a lesson from the world beyond. A living hero makes a name for himself, retaining his identity in death, not becoming one of the nameless masses of the dead, but the "great dead."

Akhilleus and Odysseus have antithetical fates, which are contrasted when they meet. Akhilleus achieves *kléos* in exchange for his *nóstos*: glory and fame in exchange for his return. His is a horizontal transcendence rather than vertical. He becomes like Dionysos, a hero-god in the Underworld. Odysseus is on the Path of Return – of vertical transcendence.

Akhilleus' fate is either *nóstos* without *kleós*, or *kleós* without *nóstos*. Odysseus attains *nóstos* with *kleós*. Akhilleus gains *Kleós Áphthiton* (Undying Glory), but Odysseus goes beyond this. There is an echo of the divine twins about the two men. One is the horseman warrior who dies and the other the intelligent cattleman who returns from the dead. Akhilleus is sunset, while Odysseus is sunrise.

Akhilleus dies gloriously on the battlefield of Troy, passing with the sun into the Underworld where he remains. Odysseus journeys through the Underworld until he reemerges reborn with the sun at dawn.

After satisfying his curiosity for knowledge, Odysseus returns to Kirke who gives him directions to Ithake. She calls him "twice dead," as he entered the Underworld when he left Troy and visited it again during the *nékyia*. While the sorceress gives him directions home, Teiresias gives him the directions to his ancestral home – to the beginning of the vertical Polar Ascent in the North.

The funeral instructions of Elpenor are very similar to the ritual to Poseidon prescribed by Teiresias, suggesting that Odysseus is to give himself a sailor's funeral in the North, far from the sea. This is a ritual death once more, meaning Odysseus would be "thrice dead" upon its completion.

Sirens, Skylla, and Kharybdis

Taking the advice of Kirke, Odysseus has his men's ears blocked up with beeswax as they approach the island of the Sirens. However, Odysseus wishes to hear the song that lures sailors to their deaths. He has the crew tie him to the mast of the ship to bear witness.

Half birds, half women, the Sirens call out to him and sing the song of Troy. He yearns to swim to the island; but as instructed, the sailors bind him even faster to the mast. They pass the island and the spell is broken.

The Sirens' island is the land of death. The harbingers of death and destruction sing the song of Troy to remind Odysseus of his past. They try to draw him to the life of his simple heroic past – to clear-cut heroism. They try to fill him with nostalgia ("return ache"). The Sirens aim to reverse the direction of return, taking the hero backwards to a lower time.

Odysseus needs to feel the pull of the past and move beyond it. He is filled with pity for lost comrades and yearning for former glories. The hero forges ahead, seeking new and greater glory as he makes his way to his true home. He fights past the debilitating nostalgia to continue on his Path of Return. Tied to the ship and the present, he works in the now.

Odysseus decides not to follow the Argonauts' path through the clashing rocks; he is no Jason, a man who failed to complete the Solar Path. Instead, he chooses to thread the narrow passage past the whirlpool Kharybdis and sea monster Skylla. As he passes the monster, she takes six of his men with her six mouths.

Skylla means "Bitch," and she is the daughter of the Underworld deity Hekate. The dog is totemic of the witch queen of the Underworld. Odysseus escapes death, but six of his men are lost in the process. These six mirror the six lost to the kyklops, as well as the six lost off each of his original twelve ships to the Kikonians.

Thrinakia

Both Teiresias and Kirke warn Odysseus not to harm the cattle on the island of Thrinakia. He tries to sail past the island, but his men plead with him to land so they can rest. As he does not want open revolt, he consents under condition they do not eat any of the cattle or flocks there.

The herds on Thrinakia (Trident Isle) belong to Kirke's father Helios Hyperion ("Sun on High"), the Titanic sun. The cattle of the sun are tended by two nymphs (who are also daughters of Helios and are untouchable). There are seven herds of cows and seven flocks of sheep, each made up of fifty head. Even though the crew swear not to eat the cattle, they are stranded on the island for a month due to contrary winds and run out of food.

Odysseus goes further inland to pray to the gods. He does so and then falls asleep. Eurylokhos convinces the men to sacrifice some cattle and feast in Odysseus' absence. Odysseus returns to find the men feasting and despairs; he is offered meat by his crew, but refuses. The men feast for six days and then set sail on the seventh.

Helios complains to Zeus and threatens to sink into the House of Hades permanently if the men are not killed. Zeus throws a thunderbolt at the ship and destroys it, killing all of the crew apart from Odysseus. He straddles the mast and is carried back to Kharybdis.

Odysseus manages to grab a root of the olive tree that grows on the rock by the whirlpool, holding on while the mast is sucked in. After several hours, Kharybdis spews out the mast and Odysseus drops onto it. He rides it for ten days until reaching the island of the nymph Kalypso.

Odysseus' men see him as aimlessly drifting into hazards. Only he sees, hears, and experiences – knows and apprehends the otherworld as it is. He consents to landing, knowing it may lead to their doom. When he sleeps, he escapes death once again. His men are foolish when they eat the cattle; they have no *nóos*, and therefore no *nóstos*.

Odysseus remains an ascetic, starving but taking no food. He does not give way to ruinous temptation that will end his return. Odysseus is able to show restraint under extreme testing, but his men perish as they are unable to do the same. He shows piety towards the gods, even when they are working against him. Odysseus is disciplined, hardy, and mystifying to his men.

Helios is immortal, but travels through the realm of death at night. He has the power to take men with him to their death at dusk, as well as resurrect them at dawn. Helios is agent of the death of Odysseus' men; he causes the destruction of the amorphous mass of companions.

However, Helios is a psychopomp and hierophant to the initiate. He thus separates the elect hero from the mass, the noble from the mob. These elect are initiated into his solar hierophany.

The hero, like the sun, can pass through the regions of death without dying. He can "return from death" without violating nature. This is because he has the prerogative of death, not the actual condition.

Thrinakia is where Odysseus achieves the certainty of solitude. After the slaughter of the Cattle of Helios, Odysseus is afloat at sea alone. Naked, wrecked, reduced to his elemental state, all excess has been stripped away: companions, past, future. Only the bare man in the present, symbolically dead, remains.

Kalypso

For seven years, Odysseus lives on Ogygia with Kalypso. She treats him like a husband, honours him, and loves him. She offers him immortality, which he refuses. He spends his time saddened, a shadow of his former self – a broken man.

While Poseidon is visiting the Aithiopians on the edge of the world, Athena approaches her father Zeus, asking him to intercede and free Odysseus. Zeus sends Hermes to instruct Kalypso to do so. The hero then fells trees and fashions a raft for himself before setting sail with food and supplies from the nymph.

After seventeen days of smooth sailing, Poseidon notices Odysseus on the sea. Poseidon wrecks the raft with a tremendous storm on the eighteenth day. Then Ino, also known as Leukothea (the White Goddess), appears.

Ino gives Odysseus a veil for protection. He ties it to himself, swimming to the shore. He throws the veil back into the ocean, makes his way to a small forest, and collapses exhausted on a bed of leaves.

Kalypso's name means "I will cover" or "I will conceal" – she is the hidden one, goddess of oblivion. Kalypso is related to the verb *kalyptō*, suggesting both darkness and death and making her an embodiment of the two. Hades – name of both the god and Underworld itself – means "the unlit" or "the unseen."

The island of Ogygia is an Underworldly paradise. It is the womblike navel of the unharvestable sea. Kalypso promises immortality and agelessness. The nymph and her island are seductive, offering a life of carefree comfort and indulgence. While Kalypso keeps him, Odysseus is both a foetus and an *eidôlon*: a shade of the dead without *nóos*, waiting to be born back into the light.

Poseidon is visiting the Aithiopians, who live at the edge of the world both at sunrise and sunset. The god is a proxy for Helios, and unable to act as his agent upon Odysseus while feasting with the people of the sun. This is when the other gods move to free Odysseus.

After ten years of watching him since Troy, Athena is finally able to help him. The psychopomp Hermes is the only Olympian able to cross into the Underworld, and is sent to bring back the ritually dead Odysseus. Athena only appears to him in Phaiakia and Ithake, as she cannot enter the Underworld fairy realm that Odysseus has been in. Hermes alone can move between worlds.

Hermes is the god closest in temperament to Odysseus, his descendent. He is the crafty trickster-magician at home outside the limits of normal life. He is god of boundaries, roads, portals, and liminal places. He is the great persuader – the herald who is clever with his words. He is the god of Odysseus.

After being given the tools to make a boat, Odysseus uses the enticements of the island (embodied in the trees) to create the vehicle of his departure. His path of hardship must continue so he can return to the North on his own terms.

Odysseus leaves the island and is twice born. He makes his journey to the liminal land of the Phaiakians. Before he arrives however, Poseidon wrecks him.

Queen of the Sea, Ino comes to Odysseus' aid as the White Goddess Leukothea. The salvation of sailors by a goddess at sea is linked to the mysteries of the Sanctuary of the Great Gods on the island of Samothrace. There, Hermes was one of the deities worshipped.

Initiates would be given a purple sash to signify their protection at sea, much like that given by Leukothea to Odysseus. This implies Odysseus is afforded the same protection as an initiate of the Samothracian mysteries. The colour purple is likewise thematic throughout the *Odyssey*, coming up again and again in descriptions.

Phaiakians

Odysseus awakes to the sound of girls washing in the river. He approaches them in his naked state and is greeted by Nausikaä, daughter of Alkinoös (king of the Phaiakians). She tells him that he is in Skheria, land of the Phaiakians – a people descended from Poseidon. She offers him help, and has him washed and clothed by her handmaids.

She then tells him to follow her to the city, but enter separately. When he reaches her house, he is to supplicate to her mother in order to be received as a guest and client. Odysseus waits in Athena's sacred grove until the girls have entered the city before following. Athena shrouds him in a protective mist and then meets him in the city as a young girl, guiding him to the palace of Alkinoös, which he enters still concealed.

He enters the main chamber and clasps the knees of Arete, wife of Alkinoös. The king raises Odysseus up and feasts him, giving him hospitality. Alkinoös promises Odysseus safe transportation home, as is the custom of the Phaiakians and their magical ships.

The next day the Phaiakians entertain Odysseus with games and dancing. Odysseus is challenged by the prince Laodamas, which angers him, causing him to show his superior athletic ability. The Phaiakians then calm him down and demonstrate their dancing skills and music. They give him many gifts.

After more feasting, Odysseus asks the minstrel to sing about the wooden horse at Troy. He weeps as the song is sung, leading Alkinoös to finally ask his name. Odysseus reveals himself, recounting the entire tale of his adventures. The Phaiakians give him more gifts, making his treasure greater than the spoils he lost from Troy. Odysseus is also offered Nausikaä as a wife by Alkinoös, though he humbly refuses.

After another day of feasting, Odysseus is put on board a Phaiakian ship with all his treasure. Boarding in silence, he lies down and sleeps while the sun sets, and the Phaiakian rowers convey him to Ithake. They arrive as the morning star is heralding dawn, placing him asleep at shore with his treasure, then return to Skheria. Odysseus awakes at sunrise.

Angered at his own people, Poseidon turns the returning ship to stone as it approaches the harbour of the Phaiakians. They are reminded of an old prophecy fortelling this would happen, and that Poseidon would next cut them off from the sea by surrounding them with mountains. The Phaiakians decide to never again transport a man to his homeland, preventing further retribution from the god.

The princess Nausikaä acts under Athena's influence to safely direct Odysseus to the place of his conveyance. The Phaiakians are not openly friendly to outsiders, so Odysseus must be shrouded in a mist by Athena as he walks through the city. This is hostile territory to Odysseus, as the Phaiakians are Poseidon's people. Skheria is his holy city.

Alkinoös' father, Nausithoös, was the son of Poseidon and Periboia, a princess of the Giants. They are kin to the gods. They are Atlanteans: southern Cosmic people sacred to Poseidon who act as ferrymen from the land of the dead.

Odysseus supplicates himself before the queen, Arete. Her name is the word *areté*, which means virtue or excellence. *Areté* is the total realisation of a hero's potential.

This is a test of Odysseus – a weighing of his excellence by its personification. He passes and is brought among the Phaiakians as a *xénos* (guest friend) by Alkinoös, whose name means "He who brings back by his might."

Odysseus is feasted, then proves himself superior in heroic ability by defeating the Phaiakians at games. He is piled with treasures and honoured, as he has proven his *bíē* (might) and *ménos* (inner fire). Odysseus then reveals himself, telling of his travels; he is once again given gifts and honours, since he has proven his *mêtis* (strategy) and *nóos* (perception).

Odysseus is offered Nausikaä as a final test. Odysseus rejects the offer of staying with them as prince. He instead chooses to head north to the land of the living, then on to Hyperborea at the northern edge of the cosmos.

The Phaiakian ship sets sail at sunset, arriving at sunrise. Odysseus does not speak on the ship, but sleeps on the bed made for him by the Phaiakians. This is his funeral bier, representing his journey from death to life.

Odysseus travels through the Underworld at night like the sun. Arriving back to light and life with sunrise, he is reborn with the dawn. His *nóos* is fully returned through his sleep, and active again when he arrives on Ithake.

The Phaiakian ship is turned to stone by Poseidon. They are no longer able to convey men back from the otherworld, lest Poseidon surround Skheria with a mountain. Contact is cut off from the mortal earth to the liminal world.

Odysseus has closed the door to the otherworld, beginning the Age of Iron. This makes him the final hero of the last Heroic Age. A new Age of Heroes will reopen the door, allowing the elect to once again travel through the realms beyond the influence of the gods, aiming to transcend them entirely.

Ithake

Odysseus wakes at sunrise, but is once again shrouded in a mist by Athena. He does not recognise Ithake. The goddess approaches him in disguise.

Spinning a tall tale, he tells her he is from Krete. The goddess laughs, revealing herself to him. She lifts the mist so he can recognise his fatherland.

Athena tells him about the suitors of his wife Penelope, and all that is happening in his house. They hide his treasure in a cave sacred to the nymphs. Then Athena disguises Odysseus as an old beggar.

Odysseus first goes to the hut of his swineherd Eumaios, and is cared for by him. He tells Eumaios he is from Krete and knows Odysseus. He discovers the swineherd has remained loyal to him, but does not reveal his identity.

Odysseus' son Telemakhos returns from visiting Menelaos and Nestor, surviving a murder attempt by the suitors. Telemakhos comes to the hut and tells the swineherd to go to the palace and inform his mother he is back in Ithake. Odysseus reveals himself to his son and they plot to defeat the suitors.

Odysseus and Telemakhos enter his palace separately, and the suitors hurl insults at Odysseus. He puts up with these and defeats another beggar in a boxing match who tries to remove him from the palace. After the suitors leave for the night, he is brought to Penelope.

He tells her a tall tale, but promises that Odysseus will be back imminently. Penelope tells him about her plan to set up a test with the bow of Odysseus and a row of axes for the suitors. Odysseus tells her it is a good idea, and that her husband will return before any of the suitors can perform the test.

Penelope instructs the old maid Eurykleia to wash the beggar's feet. Eurykleia does this, and recognises Odysseus from a distinct scar, but he keeps her quiet.

The next day, which is Apollon's feast day, Odysseus tells Telemakhos to prepare for battle. All weapons are removed from the hall and the loyal swineherd, as well as the cowherd Philoitios, are brought in on the plan. Axes are set up in a row and a bow brought out; then Philoitios fastens the palace gate, trapping everyone inside.

All of the suitors attempt to string the bow, but none are capable. Odysseus asks if he can try and – despite the protests of the suitors – gets the bow in his hands. He strings it with ease, shoots an arrow through all the axes, and nods to Telemakhos who arms himself. Odysseus shoots the lead suitor Antinoös through the throat, then reveals himself to the suitors.

What follows is a slaughter of the men by Odysseus, Telemakhos, and the two herdsmen, aided by Athena. The bodies are piled up in the courtyard, and the hall is cleansed by maids who were treacherous to Penelope. The maids are then hanged outside and the other traitor, the goatherd Melanthios, is cut to pieces while alive.

Odysseus and Telemakhos go to the farm of Lairtes, Odysseus' father. There they meet the old man, arm themselves, and await the suitors' fathers. They meet these men in battle and Lairtes kills the father of Antinoös. Then Athena stops the fight, they are all forced to put aside their feud, and Odysseus is proclaimed king once again.

Odysseus lies with control from the moment he arrives on Ithake. He doesn't lie to himself as Akhilleus does. He doesn't lie for himself in a mean way either.

Odysseus lies as a king sometimes must. He will fail if he is candid when arriving in Ithake. Through his deception, he gathers information and discovers who he can trust.

In his lying tales he conveys some fact. This is particularly the case when he speaks to Penelope, who understands secretly what he is really telling her. They speak a hidden language only they know. He gives her information regarding what has happened and what he will do.

Odysseus reveals himself to her on a subtle level, because truth and fact are different. Truth has meaning; it is intuitive, it carries wisdom. Fact does not carry deeper meaning, but is simply categorical observation. Odysseus reveals truth, not fact.

Odysseus tests the loyalty and character of all in Ithake. The suitors are urban elites in the home of a hero. They are decadent and ripe for destruction.

The closer Odysseus gets to his palace, the more like Akhilleus he becomes – an agent of vengeance, a reflection of the Iliadic condition. Odysseus must use *bíē* (might) to defeat the suitors. Without *bíē*, *mêtis* (strategy) is to no avail.

Odysseus has met death time and again. However, he has always overcome it. He must do this again in spectacular fashion to regain what is his: Sacred Kingship.

Ithake suffers while Odysseus is absent, as it is disconnected from memory. The suitors are punished for their lack of memory and respect for the heroic. The hero returns and destroys that which stands in opposition to the Age of Heroes. His fire burns away the dross which has accumulated, incinerating the degeneracy that has been allowed to creep into society. He illuminates even the darkest recesses.

The return of the hero allows for continuity between past, present, and future. It unifies time, placing the hero outside it.

The slaughter of the suitors occurs on the feast day of Apollon of the Glorious Bow. The feast of Apollon is Telemakhos' name day. Telemakhos means either "Far from Battle" or "Fighting from Afar."

Apollon is the god who "strikes from afar." Telemakhos is uninitiated at Delphoi, so he is the substitute of Apollon in the battle. Odysseus acts like Apollon, raining arrows down from afar at the suitors.

While Athena is Odysseus' personal goddess, Apollon is ancestral god of the house. Odysseus' maternal grandfather (son of Hermes) is called Autolykos. This name means "the Wolf Himself," and is an allusion to Apollon Lykeios: the Wolf God.

Autolykos lives on Parnassos, holy mountain of Apollon and the site of Delphoi. He is known as a master thief who has the skills of his father Hermes. Hermes steals the herd of his older brother Apollon as an infant, but is forgiven and loved especially by the heavenly archer. Autolykos steals the herd of the wicked king Sisyphos and teaches wrestling to Herakles.

It is Autolykos who names Odysseus, giving him an eponymous name. Odysseus is "hated" as Autolykos is "much hated by men and women all over the all-nourishing earth." Odysseus is also a wolfish thief and liar; however, his name is apotropaic – it turns away evil.

The wound identified by the nursemaid Eurykleia is from a boar on Mount Parnassos. As a youth, Odysseus visits his grandfather and goes on a boar hunt. He kills the boar after it charges and gores him. Autolykos and his sons heal him.

The wound is a significant emblem known by all in the household. It is inflicted during Odysseus' visit to dedicate his juvenile locks of hair to Apollon at Delphoi. The hunt is an initiatory experience of the *Hybriste,* a young wolf warrior. He is given a wound marking entry into manhood – the scar is his memento.

Odysseus channels this energy to slaughter the suitors. The wolf returns to find his she-wolf surrounded by hostile men. Death awaits them.

Penelope is Odysseus' complementary female counterpart. Her name means "weft-faced," implying a cunning weaver who is impossible to decode. While Odysseus only had a small inheritance, he gained himself a wife from a great family due to his own *areté* ("excellence"). The two make a formidable whole and are inseparable, even through physical separation.

In the Underworld, Agamemnon says the *kleos* (fame) of Penelope's *areté* will never perish. According to the shade of Akhilleus, Penelope is key to Odysseus' *kleos* and *nóstos* (return). Penelope preserves royalty, allowing Odysseus' return. Athena, daughter of the goddess Metis, oversees this, since *mêtis* is the necessary component of stable kingship (hence Zeus swallows the goddess Metis to ensure his steady cosmic rule).

Penelope is the personification of *mêtis*: the female ruling principle. The combination of *nóos* and *mêtis* make Odysseus (and Penelope) invincible. Odysseus defeats the suitors and Poseidon, and overcomes the *athloi* (labours) on his journey to complete his *nóstos:* his journey home from death.

Odysseus then joins with Penelope as Zeus does with Metis. He assimilates the feminine principle to become all-knowing and unsurpassable. *Mêtis* allows the sovereign to order the cosmos with his *bíē* (might).

The suitors want Penelope because she is the feminine counterpart of Odysseus – she is part of him. By obtaining her, they can take the right to rule from Odysseus. Only Odysseus is worthy of Penelope; the suitors have not proven themselves as heroes or kings, and are destined to be destroyed upon the restorative return of the true king. The chief suitor, Antinoös personifies this through his name, meaning "opposed to *nóos.*"

Penelope knows who Odysseus is all along, as she is a weaver of *mêtis*. She says to the old nurse, "Wash your lord's – age mate; and perhaps Odysseus by now has such feet – and such hands."

Penelope almost exposes Odysseus, but catches herself. She also reveals the plan to him about the bow and axes before she announces it to the suitors. Odysseus tells her this is a good idea. They work together to defeat the suitors; she knows only one man can accomplish the trick.

Penelope is the true bride, while Kirke and Kalypso are seductive dangers offering false immortality. Only by joining *mêtis* with *bíē,* and *nóos* with *ménos,* can the hero complete the Solar Path, creating the physico-spiritual vessel required in order to make the Polar Ascent. From there he can attempt the leap that takes him beyond the gods.

Ὑπερβόρειος Ὀδυσσέας
Hyperborean Odysseus

At the end of the *Odyssey* we leave Odysseus on Ithake. However, he must voyage north to fulfil the prophecy of Teiresias and appease Poseidon. This northward journey is the vertical path towards Hyperborea – the return Home.

Odysseus has northern ancestry. His maternal grandfather is Autolykos, "the Wolf Himself," suggesting Apollon, god of the Hyperboreans. Odysseus' paternal grandfather is Arkeisios, "Bear Man," a polar emblem.

According to the Telegony, Odysseus first inspects his herds on the mainland at Elis. This is the realm of Augeias, son of Helios, who was killed by Herakles. Odysseus' herds are stolen from the Titanic sun.

After being entertained by Augeias' grandson Polyxenos, Odysseus journeys north to Dodona in Northern Greece. Here he consults the Sacred Dodona Oak of Zeus. The Lord of Olympos speaks through the tree to those who seek answers. The oracle tells Odysseus he will be killed by his own son.

It is in the land of the Thesprotians that he performs the sacrifice to Poseidon. After fixing his oar in the ground he sacrifices a ram, bull, and boar. Next, Odysseus marries the queen Kallidike and has a son by her. Then he fights with Athena against Ares and a neighbouring tribe; however, this battle is broken up by Apollon. Following the death of the queen, he returns to Ithake.

The ritual of the oar is a sailor's funeral, like that of Elpenor on Kirke's island. Odysseus buries the sailor he was in order to return to the Steppe. After he returns from the *nékyia*, Kirke calls Odysseus *disthanes*: "twice-dead." Following this ritual funeral in the North, he is thrice dead and thrice born.

The sacrifice of ram, bull, and boar (known as the *trittús*) is the Greek reflex of the Indo-European tripartite sacrifice. Each animal represents a social caste. The ram is of the priests, bull of the warriors, and boar of the third estate. Odysseus goes beyond castes, returning to a purer Northern state.

The Northern winnowing prophecy of Teiresias is a vision of Home. Teiresias is reaching far back in time to the ancestral land of proto-Greeks. Odysseus returns to his true home on the Steppe. He relinquishes sea for sky so he can die in peace. Only on the Steppe can the pre-Greek god Poseidon be abated and put in his place.

Odysseus is of the North. When he was tricked into joining the Akhaians on the Trojan expedition, it was the southerner Palamedes who made him substitute land riches for sea poison. This is shown in the ploughing story, where Odysseus feigns madness and sows salt into the ground. It foreshadows Odysseus' hardship at sea away from his land.

Palamedes is a Mediterranean. He represents the South and the "civilisation" it offers. He is money, trading, and cities; he is the enemy. Palamedes promises suffering in the South, while Tiresias holds the possibility of transcendence in the North.

Odysseus is the Northern hero who adopts Southern guile in order to make his way home through hostile territory. His heart remains true, but his outward behaviour is his shield against the world he lives in until he can regain his true Northern homeland. Once he has attained the Polar transcendence, he returns to Ithake a fully realised man who has come face-to-face with Hyperborean Apollon.

His battle alongside Athena against Ares and the Brygoi tribe is ended by the appearance of the God of the North. Apollon as Wolf God is found at the beginning of the hero's path when he is initiated into the wolf pack in youth. At the end, when the hero has reached the Polar summit, he finds Apollon again. Hyperborean Apollon marks the zenith – the full illumination of the spiritual sun rising high above the Holy Mountain.

The peak of the mountain is the launchpad to take a powerful leap through the Cosmos to the centre, from which he can see the wheel of time turn. It is here, as Lord of the Centre, that the hero can sit outside time. Beyond the Cosmic cycle, he is past the gods in *atidevic metátheos*.

Odysseus does not make this leap. He reaches Hyperborea, marries the queen Kallidike ("Good Justice"), and has a son. He then returns to the mortal world.

He chooses to die by the hand of Telegonos ("Far Born"), his son by Kirke. He dies in peace, an old man who has attained a vertically transcended state. He has made the Return to Hyperborea.

Odysseus is versatile, controlled, unshakeable, flexible, and steadfast in equal measure. He is able to navigate between whirlpool and sea monster. Odysseus employs his guile to reach heroic goals. Like Hermes, he is a clever and cunning trickster.

Odysseus is *polymetis* ("many skilled"), *polymechanos* ("very ingenious"), and *polytlas* ("much-enduring"). He knows the world – he fought at Troy and travelled dimensions of existence few can imagine.

Odysseus measures himself with divine beings. Striving against gods and men, he prevails. He is the last of heroes, and his death marks the end of the Age.

Nestor (embodiment of *nóos* and semi-divine figure) does not return with Odysseus from Troy. He parts ways with him, setting him on his journey. Of all heroes, he knows only Odysseus is capable of accomplishing the last heroic act of their epoch.

His companions cross to the otherworld with him, but only Odysseus has the *nóos* to complete the *nóstos*. Throughout this journey, he is invisible to the material world. He has a non-physical state in another Cosmos.

Odysseus journeys through and against time. He is an inter-dimensional temporal traveller. He can go where the gods cannot go and do what the gods cannot do.

Odysseus appears younger and older as Athena changes him. This is because he is outside of time. He can cross the barriers of time and space due to his *nóos* and *mêtis*.

Apollon is opposed to Akhilleus, but never Odysseus. Akhilleus is never on the Polar Climb, and can only attain horizontal transcendence. Like the sun, Apollon takes Akhilleus down to the underworld, but Akhilleus is not destined to rise with the sun like Odysseus.

Helios is the antagonist of Odysseus. Odysseus understands the roles of the two solar gods. He does not set himself in opposition to the Olympian, knowing that Apollon lies at the end of the journey to the Hyperborean North.

Instead, Odysseus strives against the Titanic sun. He takes on the titanic part of his own nature. He steals the sun's cattle, the light, and his own return to life from death and darkness.

Odysseus is initiated into the mysteries of the Underworld by Kirke and Teiresias. He then begins animating the souls of the dead through necromantic ritual. He decides the order in which they come to the blood.

Odysseus completes the horizontal Solar Path, "returning from death" in the Underworld and reuniting the sacred ruler with the divine queen. He then embarks to the North, beginning the vertical Polar Ascent.

The hero who journeys into the Underworld acts as the sun. He retains his brilliant, illuminating mind while ritually dying in the darkness before being reborn into the light. Odysseus makes this return because of his exceptional *nóos*.

Odysseus only tells his story to the Phaiakians in the otherworld. When he returns to Ithake he does not tell his tale to anyone, except for Penelope in their marriage bed. The Phaiakians are closed off from the human world for helping Odysseus. This marks the end of the previous Age of Heroes and beginning of the Age of Iron.

The doorway to the realm of the Phaiakians must reopen, reconnecting the divine and human worlds and beginning the next Golden Age. Odysseus closes the gates, so his spiritual descendants must be the ones to reopen them.

The otherworld is filled with forces that counteract Olympian order. It is closed so that humans can no longer have access to the forbidden spaces and knowledge accessible only to gods. The hero must break through the barrier, against the wishes of the gods, in order to reunite with them.

Knowledge of this other cosmos that thrives outside of Zeus' order is dangerous knowledge. This invisible cosmos is where human and divine states are fluid. The hero exists in the material world sustained by Zeus' order, so he must honour the gods. By entering into the divine realm, he enlists help from the gods in order to strive against them and go beyond them.

Odysseus keeps the thought of Penelope and his return in his mind, never calling for the gods' aid, as they have abandoned him. Only Athena and Hermes offer their assistance to the hero, despite the resistance of the older gods. Odysseus struggles against the Titanic sun; through this endeavour he emulates its Underworld journey from sunset to sunrise, shedding his own titanic qualities. He is reborn a hero worthy of reintegrating his divine feminine counterpart and beginning the vertical Polar Ascent to the supreme centre in the true North.

Odysseus pushes ever forward, never looking back. Never regressing into the comfort of the past, he forges ahead creating his own destiny. To the outside world he appears as a vagabond and drifter – a "Nobody." This is his shield.

Behind this shield is a magician, a noble, a warrior. He is a Holy King in humble masquerade. He moves through the world in disguise, fighting against what is placed in his path until arriving Home.

After he has reached Hyperborea, he ceases his ascent. He does not strive further. If he did, we would not know the story. The path would not have been marked for us.

By returning to the mortal earth, Odysseus brought us the map. He is the key to it. In the coming Age of Heroes, the trail he blazed is invaluable – it shows us the way Home.

νέος γένος των ἥρώων

New Age of Heroes

Homer's tales merged into the heroic mythos, contributing their substance to a stream flowing into the deepest strata of Indo-European consciousness. We must make our deeds worthy of being added to that timeless ancestral current. We must will into existence a new Age of Heroes, rising to the standards set forth by the ancients and taking control of our Cosmic destiny.

We must form a new *āristoi* capable of ruling ourselves. We must leave the hoi polloi (masses) to their hedonistic, earthly pleasures. They cannot tread the path; that is the right of the select few, those notables who embrace the true heroic virtues. In our coming Age of Heroes, we must perform deeds and live lives worthy of being added to the stream of our ancestral mythology. We must make the gods envy us again.

It is time for us to look back to the last Age of Heroes for guidance. We must not lose ourselves in sentimentalism, or wish we were there then, but charge ever forward. Now is the time of a new Age of Heroes.

In the depths of the Age of Iron, the Age of Lead, there is no better time to pursue transcendence. For those seeking excellence through conflict, now is the time. The conditions for man have never been so oppressive.

The pressure is coming to a head. New heroes must be at the tip of the spear driving us into a new Golden Age. There, men and gods will know each other once more.

This Age of Heroes will determine whether we sink deeper into the yawning abyss of chaos, or pull ourselves up to the light. Two choices lie ahead: do what fate wills and be obstructed, or battle over the ramparts of destiny to take our fortune.

We need our Akhilleuses to hold true the purity of the Northern Way, but many will be lost as they refuse to adapt to the modern world. We need our Odysseuses to work within the framework of the present time without nostalgia, while keeping the flame of Northern Fire alive in their hearts. These heroes will make the journey home, bringing more with them and ushering in a new Golden Age.

We cannot go backwards, following the Siren song into an illusory yesteryear; our only way is forward. We must push past the dark Age of Iron and continue along the great spiral of time. We must exert our will to begin a new Age of Heroes and bring about a Golden Age, resetting the Cosmic cycle.

The authoritarian Troy of the modern world has made itself clear to us. Its walls have been constructed through the pain and suffering of generations of our predecessors. Only by stepping out of the system imposed on us by the urbanised forces of modernity can we find true value.

The heroes of the present-day warrior band must gather and fight against it. Our immortality is gained on this battlefield through our heroic conduct. We must sack Troy once again.

In this dark Age of Iron, we are in the Underworld already. The mindless shades of the dead surround us, robotically going about their automated lives. The hero drinks from the Spring of Memory and rises from the dead back to the light, bringing about a new Age of Heroes and heralding the next Golden Age.

Akhilleus gains horizontal immortality for himself, but fails to go beyond and realise the Golden Age. Odysseus shows us the Path of Return. He is the key to a map giving us the directions to return Home.

We must, like Odysseus, pass through the darkness of this Age of Iron, retaining our inner fire to illuminate the way. Only by passing through darkness and death can we return to the light. This is the essence of the Age of Heroes: striving with all our might to bring about a new Golden Age.

Odysseus' journey is deeply transformative. He coexists with divine beings and endures the toughest ordeals. He enters the invisible world on a cosmic voyage. The chosen few are able to emulate this journey, leaving the masses to become forgotten dead who feed the earth with their remains.

Mêtis is the kingly quality that opens the vision to past, present, and future, making the hero the Lord of the Centre – the turner of the wheel of time who is outside time. *Mêtis* allows the sovereign to order the cosmos. *Mêtis* is dangerous to the gods; it blurs the lines between life and death. Odysseus is both loved and hated by them, since he presents a threat.

Both *bíē and mêtis* are required of the hero seeking vertical transcendence. Without *bíē, mêtis* is powerless; in the absence of *mêtis, bíē* is disorienting. Akhilleus is all *bíē* like the kyklops, but Odysseus has a balance of both like Zeus. Zeus has the ultimate cosmic *bíē*; he consumes the goddess Metis to gain balance. He joins male and female principles.

Nóos is the knowledge of what was: the memory of past heroes. This is what opens the gates to the Underworld, allowing the return; it completes the Solar Path, propelling the hero on to begin the vertical Polar Ascent. All can enter the oblivion of the Land of the Dead, but only the elite can traverse it and leave. They do this by combining their *nóos* with the inner fire of their *ménos*.

We carry countless lifetimes of knowledge in our blood. To unlock the ancestral wisdom is the ability of a few. If this is achieved, nothing can stand in the hero's way.

The hero must undergo misery, unhappiness, toil, and hardship in order to affect the transformation of time spent in the Underworld. This Age of Iron is our Underworld. The hero weathers the storm of the Age of Lead, understanding this is vital to his own journey of transmutation.

Fire has dominion over earth as Akhilleus has power on the battlefield. Wind has dominion over water as Odysseus sails on the sea. Fire and wind are Cosmic masculine forces, while earth and water are terrestrial feminine elements.

These must be combined by the hero who attains the bride, renouncing the seductive nymph. The true female principle is the transfiguring and unifying bearer of life. This liberates and transforms if brought under the hero's Olympian dominion.

The hero on the Polar Ascent must balance fire and earth, wind and water; *bíē* and *mêtis*, *ménos* and *nóos*; masculine and feminine. The hero must prove his virility through adventure, feat, and fight. This opens the transcendent forces lying latent within him, allowing the hero to transform fire into light.

The hero who gives way to titanic material virility, becoming frenzied, is unbalanced in his Self. He becomes the Titan who wants to steal divine fire for his own purposes. This is a Promethean usurpation of power.

We meet Apollon at the beginning and end of the journey. Hermes and Athena are our guides and protectors. Only Hermes can be with us through our time in the Underworld. Athena guides and helps us in the descent and ascent.

Apollon lies at both extremes: nadir and zenith. After the solar Apollonian initiation, the hero makes a Hermetic voyage until returning to light. He then encounters Apollon again on the Hyperborean polar peaks; it is there that all sentimentalism, utilitarianism, and human rhetoric evaporate.

The Heroic Spirit awakens as an irresistible force from above. It is animated by an unstoppable will to drive ever forward and upward, overcoming all obstacles material and immaterial. From a blazing nucleus, a blinding brightness radiates out into the world. The Age of Iron is coming to a close; the Age of Heroes is upon us. The end of the night is ours, and the Golden Age cannot be ushered in without action.

Only once we have passed through the Underworld of the Age of Iron and been reborn as the sun at dawn can we reopen the gateway to Phaiakia. Then we make the journey North to ascend to the Polar Centre and rejoin the Hyperboreans, reseeding the next Golden Age. This is the essence of the Age of Heroes, and our crucial mission.

We must rise above and become the embodiment of what the rulers of the Age of Iron seek to destroy. We are not just men, but sleeping gods. Once we have entered the marvellous assembly of the Hyperboreans, we must reach beyond them. Beyond the gods, time, and space, we must continue ascending outside conditioned material existence to the pure transcended *atidevic* state of *metátheos*.

Odysseus acts as a *bodhisattva*: one who turns back from the final stage of attainment. He returned from Hyperborea so the heroes of today can follow in his footsteps, returning our people to the Golden Age. He shows us that the responsibility of an enlightened few is to come back and retrieve others.

We must not only return to Hyperborea, but return Hyperborea to us. We must first reinstate the Golden Age within ourselves before it can be externally manifested in the Cosmos. Only then can we bring about a new Age of Heroes.

Heroic Code of Honour

In the coming Age of Heroes, the elect must adopt an appropriate code of honour. The actions and choices of the hero look like they are non-moral, even immoral from an outward perspective. To those with an honour code this is not so, as they understand intrinsically there is no morality other than honour.

This may seem overly simple at first, but there is a complex set of strictures at the heart of honour. These precepts are unbending, and will undoubtedly test one's resolve.

Aidōs is shame, disgrace, and fear of disgrace. It is the hero's sense of propriety. Aversion to *aidōs* is the strongest moral force.

Aretḗ is virtue and excellence. It is the total realisation of the hero's potential.

Aristeíā is prestige. It is the pinnacle of action. It is the hero's excellence on the battlefield.

Atē means "error" or "delusion." It implies wrongness and wickedness.

Bíē means "might." It is a prerequisite to *kléos*: a vital component of the hero. Without *bíē*, man is not a hero. *Bíē* can also be harmful if not tempered with *dikē* (justice), leading to rash, violent, often irreversible decisions.

Daímōn is an unspecified superhuman force. It is an unknown god or gods.

Kléos is fame, glory, or news. It is what the hero seeks: a name that will live on after his death.

Kûdos is the glory of victory – the golden lustre of those who win. It is the divine mark of the successful.

Mênis is anger. This is not a bad trait, but can easily give way to *khólos* (rage). It is a whole-body reaction driving men to violent speech and deed.

Ménos means impulse. It is the inner fire of the hero: the feeling of strength and braveness. It is a single vitality expressed through somatic and psychic vigour. *Lússā, mênis,* and *khólos* are manifestations of *ménos*. *Lússā* is the heat of *ménos* raised too high; it is a rabid, animal-like state.

Mêtis is strategy, cunning, planning, and clever artifice.

Némesis is a feeling of outrage – righteous indignation.

Nóos is vision, but not sight. It is recognition of meaning in things perceived or imagined.

Psykhê is the eschatological soul. Its only function is to leave the man upon death.

Thumós means "spirit," "breath soul," or "life soul." It is used to mean "heart." It is an organ of feeling.

Tīmê is honour. It is the value placed on the hero by his peers. It also means status, price, and penalty. Honour must also be given to the gods in order to avoid *hubris* (pride), which offends the gods.

The hero balances his *ménos* and *nóos*, his *bíē* and *mêtis*. Using inner fire and insight in equal measure, as well as might and strategy in harmony, he unifies these forces within his *thumós*. Externalising them, he becomes a transcendent hero.

The true hero values *tīmê*, shunning *aidōs* and *atē*. He seeks *kûdos* and *kléos*, looking to attain *aretê* through his *aristeíā*.

Be the hero. Seek that which is higher and reject that which is lower. Strive to transcend, moving ever upward on the vertical path of ascent.

AGE OF HEROES

Was written by Tom Billinge.

Learn more about Tom at **TomBillinge.com**.

If you enjoyed this book, consider reading
Undying Glory: The Solar Path of Greek Heroes and *WarYoga*,
also by Tom Billinge.

Watch for future releases by Tom and other authors from
Sanctus Europa Press.

Sanctus Europa is a crusade to defend European spirituality.

Join our holy campaign at **SanctusEuropa.com**.

LUX IN TENEBRIS

Made in the USA
Monee, IL
03 July 2023

38579417R10142